MATERNAL BONDING

Wladyslaw Sluckin, Martin Herbert
and Alice Sluckin

BASIL BLACKWELL

First published 1983
Basil Blackwell Publisher Limited
108 Cowley Road, Oxford OX4 1JF, England

A Grant McIntyre book

British Library Cataloguing in Publication Data

Sluckin, Wladyslaw
    Maternal bonding.
    1. Mother and child   2. Infants
    I. Title   II. Herbert, Martin
    III. Sluckin, Alice
    155.4'22   BF723.P25

ISBN 0-631-13358-5
ISBN 0-631-13359-3   Pbk

Typesetting by Getset (BTS) Ltd
Printed in Great Britain

MATERNAL BONDING

CONTENTS

1

Infantile and maternal attachments

Every so often a psychological theory escapes the confines of sober academic debate associated with professional conferences or learned journals, and enters the wider public arena (and consciousness) by way of extensive publicity in the mass media. In recent times, the theory of 'maternal bonding' has enjoyed (or suffered) the somewhat unrestrained discussion characteristic of newspaper items, magazine features and television comment. What is the reader or viewer – especially the expectant young mother – to make of the interesting but also sometimes disturbing ideas surrounding this concept of a maternal bond?

How authoritative are the far-reaching claims of the significance of the mother's early skin-to-skin contact with her baby for its present and future well-being? How real are the psychological dangers of a separation of mother from her newborn infant in its early days of life in the event that the baby is actually ill and must go into intensive care? Indeed at a more basic level, what is meant by the term 'maternal bond' to which so many commentators allude rather blandly, but which so few try to define with any precision?

Does the expression imply that there is a tie between a mother and her child which is unique to females – a special relationship which fathers cannot attain, no matter how much they love their offspring? And that raises a further question: is the maternal bond to be equated broadly with the phrase 'mother love'? Or is it a technical term like the word 'attachment' in the literature on infant-to-mother attachments? The public could be excused for accepting the theory of maternal bonding in an uncritical manner, as received wisdom. It is usually presented as a confident synthesis of ideas – a doctrine with a firm knowledge base, derived from painstaking research. But is this really the case? These are but some of the issues to be examined in this book.

Granted, the questions posed above are difficult enough to answer; and none more so than the one concerning the meaning of the words 'maternal bond'. Both theoreticians and practitioners seem to use the term in various ways. This is hardly surprising as they often seem to assume, or imply, that it is synonymous with maternal love; and love is surely one of the most elusive words in the language. It is crucial to attempt the admittedly difficult task of providing a technical and operational definition of love, but that is far from being the whole story. After all, there are many kinds of love: a mother's love for her child, the child's for its parents, the love of a child for a child, and love between adults — to give only a few examples.

It is necessary to distinguish between love and affectional feelings. In each case of love mentioned above (and in others) love is but a part of one individual's feelings of affection for another person. The concept of affectional feelings is *broader* than, but includes, love.[1]* Affectional feelings of mother for child show themselves outwardly as maternal attachment; affectional feelings of infant for adult manifest themselves as infantile attachment; and so on. This book is primarily about maternal attachment, but also more generally about parental attachment. It is important at the outset to draw a clear distinction between infantile attachment on the one hand and maternal attachment on the other.

Behaviour which is characteristic of infantile attachment may readily be observed in its many forms in human children, as well as in the young of birds and non-human mammals. Ducklings, goslings and chicks following a person have often been photographed, filmed and televised; they have been seen by many. Although normally attached to their natural mother, such hatchlings can become attached with ease to a foster parent or — in the laboratory — to a moving inanimate object, or to a flickering light, or, somewhat less readily, to a salient stationary figure. This type of early learning is known as imprinting.[2] The newborn of mammalian species capable of locomotion soon after birth — as are most herbivores such as horses, cattle or deer — also appear to form attachments by exposure to figures in their immediate environment, which normally are their mothers. Other young mammals, including infra-human primates, such as monkeys and apes, show strong ties to their

*References are to be found at the end of each chapter.

mothers and sometimes also to other individuals; although it is a matter of debate whether those attachments can be ascribed mainly to imprinting-like exposure learning.

Regardless of how acquired, the specific attachment of a young animal to a particular adult or adult-substitute is known as *infantile attachment*. Naturally, just as an infant can be attached to its mother, so also a mother can be attached to her infant or infant-surrogate. This type of attachment is known as *maternal attachment*. Before plunging into the subject-matter of the book, it will be worth while to say just a little about infantile attachment because of certain parallels between the two types of attachment and the two affectional systems.

There is a vast literature on the subject of the affectional ties of human infants to their parents, particularly in the context of maternal deprivation. The most influential writings have been those of John Bowlby.[3] In the briefest outline, his early view was that the child's strong attachment to its mother was necessary for normal, healthy development: and conversely, that deprivation of maternal affection, or protracted maternal separation, was liable to result in maladjustment which could show itself in a variety of ways, including delinquency. Bowlby's later view, following an examination of further research findings, was that the child's separation from its caretaker did not inevitably result in the maladjustment of the child; but at the same time, a long-lasting absence of a mother-figure before the age of about five years did greatly interfere with the child's healthy psychological development. The debate concerning infantile attachment and maternal deprivation has continued. Since about 1970 some very useful general appraisals have become available of maternal deprivation effects, as well as of current theories of infantile attachment.[4]

It is instructive to consider, if only extremely briefly, some practical consequences of the Bowlbian view. Since child-to-parent uninterrupted attachment was seen as very important for the psychological well-being of the child, the impact of child-parent separations had to be, whenever possible, minimized. Accordingly, from the 1950s onwards, children's wards in hospitals were opened to visiting relatives. Previously, it had been believed that sick children who saw their parents became unnecessarily upset. The new view was that it would be better for children to show emotion than to be quietly miserable through continued separation from their loved ones. Thus, the apparent harshness of hardly allowing children in hospital to receive visitors was done away with. The positive influence of Bowlby and others expressing similar views extended also into another sphere. Earlier on, children in institutional care had been herded together in large establishments, each catering for perhaps hundreds of children. The new ideas demanded that the size of the institutions be drastically reduced. Children were now being put into family-sized cottage homes, each run jointly by a foster mother and a foster father. In time it was realized that the appalling damage to young children so vividly described earlier by Spitz[5] was not the result of maternal deprivation as such but was due to lack of personal contact and stimulation in bad institutions.

However, side-by-side with these social improvements, certain less desirable developments were in evidence. During the last war nurseries for preschool children were established to enable mothers to contribute to the war effort in factories, offices and elsewhere. Since separation from the mother was now thought to be undesirable for young children, war-time nurseries were being closed down. This penalized some youngsters, depriving them of enriching experiences outside the home. It also greatly inconvenienced those mothers who still went to work and who now had to make their own private, and often less adequate, arrangements for child minding. Many parents among the better-educated tended to think that even short mother – infant separations could harm their children psychologically. Such mothers felt anxious or guilty whenever they had to leave their children for a day or so, and were reluctant to make arrangements for substitute care. As a result of continuing research, we nowadays consider that the mother's anxiety and guilt feelings were exaggerated and that well-run nurseries for young children have their very valuable role to play in a modern society.

So much for infantile attachment; we shall be considering at some length in Chapter 5 the consequences of some contemporary ideas about maternal attachment. We shall then be fully assessing in a similar manner both the advantageous and deleterious effects in practice of the current notions concerning maternal attachment and mother-to-infant 'bonding'; but we shall adumbrate this assessment shortly in the present introductory chapter.

Compared with the literature on infantile attachment, the sum-total of what has been written on maternal attachment is quite small. Furthermore, while this is being written, there has been no comprehensive review of this field other than in one paper in a learned journal by the authors of this book.[6] And yet there are plenty of ideas about maternal instinct, maternal behaviour, maternal attachment and maternal bonding 'floating about'. These ideas influence day-to-day practice in maternity hospitals, homes and nurseries; they influence decisions made in courts of law (e.g. whether a child is to be taken away from its parents, or which of the contesting parents is to be given custody); they influence the advice to young mothers given by doctors, nurses and social workers; they influence what young mothers think and do and feel. So much for our justification for writing this book.

We shall be paying special attention in the book to one set of ideas which we shall call the critical-period bonding view of maternal attachment, or more simply, the bonding doctrine. Most briefly put, the view is that immediately after the birth of her baby the mother must be made to hold and fondle it in order to become emotionally tied to the baby; for if she is not, her bond or attachment to the child will be inadequate, which could have harmful long-lasting consequences. We shall consider in Chapter 2 how this view has evolved and emerged.

Let us, however, for a moment see how the bonding doctrine has influenced some kinds of day-to-day practice. On the positive side, this view has discouraged the unnecessary and sometimes distressing separation of newborn babies from their mothers, which until not long ago had been customary in maternity hospitals. The bonding view has also encouraged paediatricians to allow mothers to care for low-birth-weight infants sooner rather than later; this appears to do no physical harm to such infants, to save on baby care costs, and to make mothers feel that they are actively helping the baby through a difficult period.[7] These humanizing effects have been, however, counter-balanced, and sometimes more than counterbalanced, in a number of ways.[7]

Misguided ideas about good early mothering held by some nurses have led in some cases to the harassment of those mothers who in the early stages appear to have difficulty in relating to their infants. Such mothers can be made to feel inadequate or guilty or depressed or resentful; and none of these feelings is conducive to the gradual development of maternal love and attachment and good mothering. In a different vein the bonding view has been used in explaining child maltreatment; for example the abusing mother is said to be inadequately bonded to her abused child. The too-ready acceptance of such views by some social workers, psychologists and psychiatrists has tended to inhibit a broader and more thorough analysis of all the circumstances surrounding the given cases of child abuse; and this in turn may have prevented the most appropriate remedial action from being adopted. As mentioned earlier, we shall be returning to a more detailed consideration of all such matters in Chapter 5.

Before we reach that stage of the book, the nature of the critical-period bonding doctrine will be examined in detail in Chapter 3; and all the evidence, for and against the bonding view, will be fully and carefully examined in Chapter 4. After looking at the implications of the theory for practice in Chapter 5, we shall turn in Chapter 6 to broader issues: we shall survey the state of knowledge with regard to the evolutionary development of, what has been called, maternal instinct; we shall consider what is known about learning processes in order to try to understand how people come to be so strongly attached to their own offspring, to their adopted children, and even their grandchildren and their friends' children. Finally we shall try to bring all the threads together in Chapter 7 in an attempt to learn some severely practical lessons about parental actions and attitudes. This then is our programme.

References

1 Harlow, H.F. (1958) 'The nature of love', *American Psychologist*, **13**, 673 – 85.
   Harlow, H.F. (1971) *Learning to Love* (San Francisco: Albion).
2 Sluckin, W. (1972) *Imprinting and Early Learning* (London: Methuen).
   Hess, E.H. (1973) *Imprinting: Early Experience and Developmental Psychobiology of Attachment* (New York: Van Nostrand).
3 Bowlby, J. (1951) *Maternal Care and Mental Health* (Geneva: World Health Organisation).
   Bowlby, J. (1969). *Attachment and Loss: Vol. 1, Attachment* (London: Hogarth Press).
4 Rutter, M. (1972) *Maternal Deprivation Reassessed* (Harmondsworth: Penguin).
   Rajecki, D.W., Lamb, M.E. and Obmascher, P. (1978) 'Toward a general theory of infantile attachment', *The Behavioral and Brain Sciences*, **3**, 417 – 64.
5 Spitz, R.A. (1946) 'Anaclitic depression', *Psychoanalytic Study of the Child*, **2**, 313 – 42.

6 Herbert, M., Sluckin, W. and Sluckin, A. (1982) 'Mother-to-infant "bonding" ', *Journal of Child Psychology and Psychiatry*, **23**, 205 – 21.
7 Professor David Davies (Chinese University of Hong Kong; formerly, Department of Child Health, Medical School, University of Leicester) – personal communication.

2

Postnatal care of infants

The bonding doctrine is concerned with (a) the contact between the newborn infant and its mother and (b) the long-term influence of this on the mother-to-infant attachment. The nature of the early child care – the form it takes – is said to be of crucial importance for the development of the relationship between the mother and her child. It will not surprise the reader that the care-giving precepts inherent in the bonding view are but a recent stage in the long history of ideas and practices of child care. From time to time new thoughts on the handling of neonates and new practices have emerged. Yet with the passing of time new ideas become old-fashioned; they fade away, perhaps to reappear later in new guises, they undergo reformulations, they alter in their emphases, they re-emerge, they go out of fashion again. Not many years ago a remarkable book came out, citing the writings over the last five hundred years or so about the theories and practices of child care, including the care of newborn infants.[1] Among other things, the close connection is brought out between the changing ideas about child care and the history of a wide range of social attitudes. Generally, new styles of care-giving are an integral part of economic and social developments on a broad front.

Throughout the history of mankind until relatively recent times, infant mortality was very high indeed. Child care of the newborn has tended to be primarily directed towards the preservation of life, although various misguided practices have sometimes rendered ineffective the efforts of all those attending childbirth. Very broadly speaking, the natural mother would sooner or later hold and suckle the baby. At some stage mother and baby would be washed clean. In Europe and in many other parts of the world – but certainly not everywhere – young babies were traditionally swaddled; this provided some protection for the helpless infant, and therefore by and

8

large probably did more good than harm. At various times these basic early routines − giving the baby to the mother, washing the baby, putting it into swaddling clothes and so on − were a matter of debate and to some degree subject to fashion. It is these early routines that must in the first place be the object of our interest.

Indications of very old child care practices may be found in the writings of the ancients: Egyptians, Jews, Greeks and Romans; and also in the written heritages of India, China and other lands. The Middle Ages, too, produced much literature, especially in Arabic in the Middle East and in Latin in Central and Western Europe, providing many pointers to the various types of care then given to newborn infants. There are still some beliefs, and not a few superstitions, in different localities of Europe and Britain that clearly have their roots in the Middle Ages and even the pre-Christian days. Washing the baby has always been accorded much attention. Ritual immersions in water were in the ancient world thought to be a means of not only bodily but also of spiritual purification. Forms of baptism already existed in the pre-Christian era. The Church ritualized the practice and assigned it a special significance. The 'bath water' blessed by the priest was holy and was believed to shield the child from evil. It is not altogether surprising that at a time when infant mortality was very high indeed, superstitious beliefs as to what brought good luck or bad luck were widespread.[2] For instance in some parts of the country, to weigh a child before its first birthday was thought unlucky; fingernails had to be bitten or broken off rather than cut. Magical charms worn by babies to bring good luck were still popular in the eighteenth century.

Many of the old beliefs die hard. Dr Marie Stopes, for instance, writing in 1920, refers to the 'gossipy opinion that women who are spared the full torture of childbirth do not have equally passionate love for the child'.[3] How much of the advice given today on care-giving, discipline and child-rearing in general is at that level? In particular, it may be asked whether some of the views current at the present time as to what is necessary to establish or enhance the love of the mother for her newborn infant are − to use the Marie Stopes phrase − but a gossipy opinion.

Gradually, scientific advancement, and particularly a better understanding of human physiology and the causes of diseases, have brought about an era of relative enlightenment. It is difficult to put a date to its beginning, but perhaps the end of the seventeenth century in Europe may be considered to be the dawn of the modern age of science. At any rate, the immediate precursors of many recent and present-day ideas concerning post-partum child care may be discerned at that time. The new ideas had to do not only with child care but also related to the way children were perceived, for example as possible objects of study. In the wake of industrialization, extended families, with grandparents, aunts and uncles all living close-by, were becoming less common; the typical family was now nuclear, that is consisting just of mother, father and their children. Mother now tended to be the sole care-giver, and there was some moral pressure upon her to be a good mother. The early utterances, from which current opinions and debates have descended, may be found in the writings of a variety of authors, ranging from philosophers and moralists to practising physicians. The men of letters, as well as those offering practical guidance, often questioned the merits of the earlier traditional care-giving procedures and not infrequently used strong words to say what they regarded as best for the neonate and for its mother.

We can observe four stages, not necessarily clearly demarcated from one another, in the development of thought in this regard. First, there is the stage of the new enlightenment, mentioned above, which preceded, was contemporaneous with and followed the traumatic events of the American War of Independence and the French Revolution. Second, there is the era of the relative political and social stability in the nineteenth century, and a rapid progress in the medical sciences leading to a sharp drop in infant mortality and, at the same time, a stress on a series of rules surrounding perinatal events. Third, we see a revolt, beginning in the twenties and thirties of the present century, against the rigid Victorian values, attitudes and practices. And finally, we come to modern times and the current debate as to what is best for the baby, and especially for the mother, in the early hours and days after the birth has taken place. We shall now say something about each of the first three stages and then attempt to prepare the ground for the full discussion of the fourth stage in the subsequent chapters.

The view that it is the day-to-day experiences which are largely responsible for moulding the personality of the infant into that of the adult has been called environmentalism; it contrasts with the nativist view which ascribes personality to inborn characterists.

Early on, some eminent British philosophers, exemplified by John Locke, and a little later, French writers around the time of the French Revolution, typified by Jean-Jacques Rousseau, held strongly environmentalist views. Locke thought that one could usefully exercise strict control over the infant's environment and thereby make the infant into a fitter adult; this could be achieved by toughening the infant, e.g. by exposing it to all the rigours of nature such as cold, wind, sunshine and irregular feeding. Rousseau, however, advocated a rather gentler regime: the newborn should be bathed not in cold but in warm water; and as the child grew stronger the temperature should be gradually lowered until eventually cold baths only would be allowed. Rousseau also argued vehemently against the swaddling of infants on the ground that swaddling interfered with normal development by artificially restraining the infant's movements. Generally, as an environmentalist, he attached much importance to good mothering.

Before long medical books were expressing similar views. A medical handbook widely read in Britain and the United States some 200 years ago listed a number of rules for infant care. According to these, the mother should suckle her own child but should not overfeed it, the infant should be kept clean but not excessively warm, it should be allowed some exercise, and so on. On the whole the impression one forms is that the regime advocated was a nice mixture of sternness and permissiveness.[1]

As we see it now, there is nothing very striking about this kind of guidance to infant care. However, seen against the background of earlier ideas and practices, the type of advice then offered was remarkably humane. For life had been very harsh for newborn infants in Western Europe up to that time. In France, in the seventeenth and eighteenth centuries prosperous families in the cities commonly 'farmed out' their newborn babies for some months or years to wet nurses in the country.[4] In Britain unwanted infants were often abandoned to perish in the open, while some were placed in foundling hospitals. Even the well-to-do sometimes disposed of unwanted babies by sending them away into the countryside to be lodged in 'baby farms', as these places were called.[1]

While it was now recommended that the mother should suckle her newborn infant, it should be noted that among the well-to-do, at least up to the end of the eighteenth century, the wet nurse often played a more important role in the life of the baby immediately after birth than the baby's natural mother. Poor women often abandoned their own offspring to suckle the children of the rich. It may be wondered to what extent these wet nurses became 'bonded' to their charges. Another question is how the mothers themselves felt about their wet-nursed infants, how loving towards them they were, and how much they were, or were not, attached to their children.

In the nineteenth century well-off ladies were often advised to stay in bed and rest for several weeks after giving birth. It may well be that this practice helped to reduce the high incidence of illness then prevalent in women during confinement. As perinatal morbidity and mortality in women and infants declined at the turn of the century, lengthy confinements to bed ceased to be customary. Not everyone thought highly of this change in custom. Marie Stopes expressed bitter regret in 1920 that the long, post-partum stays in bed were no longer practised.[3]

Attitudes towards early child care during the period of history which pre-dated the remarkable drop in infant mortality in the advanced countries towards the end of the last century were on the whole not favouring a rigid discipline. Admittedly, a cold bath early in life seems harsh, and giving the newborn infant to the wet nurse now appears to be a little unfeeling. Nevertheless, strict rules were not a feature of post-natal child care policy or practice. Rapid progress of the medical sciences changed all that. High infant mortality was strikingly reduced by hygiene which prevented infection. No wonder that cleanliness was now thought to be next to godliness.

Cleanliness required discipline, and practising discipline was aided by regularity in all child care arrangements. Thus, by the end of the last century the advice given to young mothers and to nurses began to stress the advantages of regularity in eating, sleeping, bathing, bowel movements, physical exercise and everything else. As a consequence of this, feelings tended to be disregarded and, indeed, had to be disregarded to a high degree: mother was not supposed to pick up her baby just because it cried, she was not expected to cuddle her baby simply because she felt like it, and so on. Early this century bottle-feeding was becoming quite common; it, too, had to follow certain rules of hygiene and regularity. It may well be asked whether such highly structured regimes interfered with the normal mother-infant interactions, especially at the emotional level. The high priest of this type of infant care early this century was Dr Truby King. His views continued to be highly influential at least until the Second World War.[5]

Truby King strongly recommended breast feeding, if at all possible. He did not mince his words. 'A woman's milk is not her own. It is created for the baby, and the first duty of the mother is to ensure, by foresight, a proper supply of the only perfect food – the baby's birthright.' He advocated for the baby an 'abundance of pure cool outside air flowing fresh day and night'. He thought — wrongly, paediatricians now tell us – that warmth is not beneficial to babies, except premature ones. As for washing the baby, he said 'bath and dress very quickly – no dawdling'. Above all, he called for regularity, for instance, 'regularity of feeding, with proper intervals and no food between meals'. With regard to bowel action, Truby King said in his book, in thick print: 'Don't let 10 o'clock in the morning pass without making baby's bowels move, if they have not moved in the previous 24 hours.' And he did say something about mothering which has a more modern ring about it. 'Proper mothering and handling of a baby are essential for the best growth and development. No woman is a perfect born-mother – she has to learn how.' Truby King's concern was for the physical well-being of the baby. He did not express any views on what was good for the mother: for her emotional satisfaction, for the growth of her love for the child, for things which could eventually benefit the child via the mother's behaviour towards it.

Gradually, a reaction began to set in against the Truby King type of approach to early infant care. There were many influences afoot from the 1930s onwards in the direction of increased latitude and greater concern for the mother's feelings. One of those influences was Dr Grantly Dick-Read; his central interest lay in childbirth itself; and in relation to it he advocated a set of new rules, a new type of discipline. However, Dick-Read also had some new and liberal thoughts on the events immediately following childbirth.[6] He was not only, like Truby King, strongly in favour of breast feeding; he also advised that the newborn baby be put to the breast at the earliest possible opportunity after the umbilical cord had been cut. He favoured this course of action even though there is no milk secreted by the mother's breasts immediately after birth, only a thick fluid called colostrum. The view held by Dick-Read and his followers was that the early direct contact of mother and baby was good for them both. The benefit derived by the mother was said to be physiological (e.g. facilitated lactation) as well as psychological. The latter benefit lay in giving the mother a sense of achievement and an emotional release.

At this point the reader may wish to know what modern scientific studies have to say about these changing beliefs. Are they for the most part but fads and fashions? Which of them, if any, are sound and likely to endure. Regretfully, in order not to be sidetracked from our main theme, we must postpone commenting on such questions until Chapter 7. For the present, we should pay special attention to another of Dick-Read's tenets, one which brings us more directly to the emergence of the bonding doctrine. We are referring to his advocacy of the practice of 'rooming-in'.

Rooming-in means that the newborn baby is kept in the same room as the mother; the two are together in one room so that the mother can constantly see her baby, and herself attend to its needs as far as is practicable. This practice had been standard in American hospitals up to the turn of the century. However, epidemics of diarrhoea, respiratory infections and the like among newborn infants led subsequently to stricter isolation arrangements of babies in separate wards. Special units for premature babies were also being set up. All these new arrangements reduced contact between mothers and their babies to a minimum.[7] Thus, on both sides of the Atlantic the Truby King type tradition prevailed until a reaction against it began to set in in the nineteen-thirties, when, among other things, rooming-in became respectable once again.

One feature of this reaction was a hostility towards hospital nurseries. Dick-Read considered them undesirable because they were thought to hinder a healthy development of mother-to-infant relationships. The practice of keeping the mother and her newborn baby together – it was said – should be re-adopted not only in private homes but also in maternity hospitals. The idea has steadily caught on. Recently some paediatricians have tied this idea to the bonding doctrine; without rooming-in – it is claimed – mother-to infant bonding is difficult to achieve.[8] It is clear, however, that there is no need to provide a justification for rooming-in in this way; indeed, it is misleading to do so. Suffice it to say that rooming-in in normal circumstances is a sensible, humane and sound practice. As for Dick-Read's views on post-natal baby-care methods, including close contact between mother and baby, it may be said that his influence was in the direction of an altogether less restrictive regime than that prescribed by the Truby King school of thought.

Professional and public opinion in the early post-war years was steadily moving away from the disciplinarian approach to the mothering of young babies. A very influential voice in America was that of Dr Benjamin Spock. In his manual published in 1945 he strongly favoured the 'rooming-in plan'. He argued that under this arrangement the mother would learn a great deal about her baby's hunger patterns and other rhythms, such as sleep and bowel movements. Instead of regular fixed-hour feeds, 'self-demand' breast or bottle feeding was now considered to be best for the baby. The father would be allowed, and even expected, to participate in all the baby-care activities.[9] The idea of rooming-in seemed at that time in the United States to be quite revolutionary; in fact, it only meant a return to what had been commonly done before the Truby King practices became firmly established. Spock freely acknowledged that his teaching would be difficult to put into practice in hospitals; it certainly required a departure from the then customary attitudes and administrative arrangements.

In the early post-war years Spock's sentiments led and reflected the post-Truby King liberalization of child care. Later, in the fifties and sixties there was much concern expressed for the mother's feelings during the birth of her baby, and especially during the hours, days and weeks immediately following. Dr Winnicott, an influential Freudian child psychiatrist, pleaded for a change of attitude towards infant care for the sake of everybody's mental health.[10] Regular feeding, he conceded, is convenient, but feeding on demand is more natural, healthier and more satisfying to baby and mother. The mother is disadvantaged when the baby is handed to her only at feed-times. It is better for her emotional well-being that she should watch her infant as it lies by her side, as it rests in her arms and as it feeds at her breast. Early and frequent contact with her baby gives the mother the necessary reassurance that all is well. However, a muted note of severity, of new strictness perhaps, may be detected in the advice that is proffered. For Winnicott suggests that the mother should regard getting to know her baby as an urgent matter. It was said to be urgent because it provided the necessary solid foundation for the developing mother – child relationship.

About a decade later a new gloss was put on the matter of mother-neonate contact by the French doctor, Frederick Leboyer. Like Dick-Read, Leboyer was primarily interested in the birth event; but whereas Dick-Read focused attention on the mother, Leboyer was more concerned with the baby.[11] Both, however, strongly advocated putting the newborn infant on to the mother's skin. Leboyer's advocacy of certain procedures at childbirth is in his book presented in a highly dramatized fashion. What he actually recommends is, however, not so very drastic: subdued light, quiet, a little delay in the cutting of the umbilical cord, placing the newborn in warm, body-temperature bath-water and so on. To anyone interested in the bonding doctrine, the most significant feature of Leboyer's teaching is his emphasis on the beneficence of post-partum skin-to-skin contact between the baby and the mother; but nothing is actually said about bonding.

Ever since the reaction set in to the Truby King approach to infant care, voices have been raised against separating newborn infants from their mothers. This change of outlook was partly prompted by simple humanitarian considerations. Rooming-in was also thought to be desirable from the viewpoint of the infant's healthy emotional development by influential writers such as John Bowlby.[12] And, as we have already seen, early contact with her infant was considered to be advantageous to the mother. In any case, the tendency was now for more contact between mother and baby than in earlier times; for earlier on, working class families were large, so that each child's contact with its mother was of necessity somewhat restricted; and among the middle classes some of the child's contacts were with the nanny (or even the wet nurse) rather than the mother.

More lately, skin-to-skin contact between the mother and her infant has been strongly urged in some quarters, and has come to be regarded as almost imperative. This has set the scene for the advent of the bonding view, which has come to provide a full justification and a seemingly compelling reason for the early mother – infant contact; it was now claimed that this contact was necessary if the mother was to develop a true and strong and lasting attachment to her baby. Thus the bonding view came onto the scene to justify a good practice. But is that kind of justification really needed? Above all, what is the evidence supporting the bonding doctrine? The next two chapters are devoted, first, to an inquiry into the nature and implications of the doctrine, and, then, to a critical review of all the empirical evidence germane to it.

References

1 Beekman, D. (1977) *The Mechanical Baby* (New York: Meridan).
2 Ash, R. *et al.* (1977) *Folklore, Myths and Legends of Britain*. (Pleasantville, N.Y.: Reader's Digest Association).
3 Stopes, M. (1920) *Radiant Motherhood* (London: Putnam).
4 Badinter, E. (1981) *The Myth of Motherhood* (London: Souvenir Press).
5 King, F.T. (1913) *Feeding and Care of Baby* (London: Macmillan).
6 Dick-Read, G. (1942) *Childbirth without Fear* (London: Heinemann).
7 Klaus, M.H. and Kennell, J.H. (1970) 'Mothers separated from their newborn infants', *Pediatric Clinics of North America*, **17**, 1015 – 37.
8 O'Connor, S., Vietze, P.M., Sherrod, K.B., Sandler, H.M. and Altemeier, M.A. (1980) 'Reduced incidence of parenting inadequacy following rooming-in', *Pediatrics*, **66**, 176 – 82.
9 Spock, B. (1945) *The Common Sense Book of Baby and Child Care* (New York: Duell, Sloan & Pearce).
10 Winnicott, D.W. (1957) *The Child and the Family* (London: Tavistock Publications).
11 Leboyer, F. (1975) *Birth without Violence* (London: Wildwood House).
12 Bowlby, J. (1953) *Child Care and the Growth of Love* (Harmondsworth: Penguin Books).

3

The Bonding Concept

We have seen in the preceding chapter how liberalizing ideas in the field of child-care, as elsewhere, can become oppressive when elevated into prescriptive dogmas. This was so in the case of the maternal deprivation hypothesis,[1] and history appears to be repeating itself with the maternal bonding doctrine.

Sadly, practice *is* tending to become doctrinaire (see Chapter 5). The eminently sensible and humane idea of allowing a mother and her new baby to get to know one another by early, frequent and intimate social interaction becomes intrusive when the permissive 'ought' of physical contact is replaced by an authoritarian 'must'. The mother *must* have physical contact with her infant (and presumably experience appropriate feelings) immediately after birth, otherwise something disastrous will happen, or − rather − not happen! She may not become bonded to her child. As Vesterdal puts it:[2]

. . . the mother-child interaction may be stopped at the very beginning by separation of the child from the mother. This will happen if the baby has to be taken to a special-care unit of the hospital immediately after birth because of prematurity or some serious illness. Also in these cases the mother may feel disappointed with the baby or with herself, and there will of course be enormous difficulties in establishing contact between mother and child, with the result that she may feel alienated towards it and a normal bonding cannot develop . . .

And it is no ordinary relationship which is referred to by the expression 'normal bonding'. When all goes well an attachment is being cemented between a mother and her baby, a relationship implying unconditional love, self-sacrifice and nurturant attitudes which, for the mother's part, will last a lifetime.

Small wonder that paediatricians and social workers, not to mention young mothers (who soon hear of these matters from the media) are concerned, especially if there is truth in what might be called the 'ethological' account of the events leading to the bonding of mother to child.

This version, in its most unrestrained form encountered in professional seminars and talks rather than scientific papers, suggests that particular events occurring during the first few hours and days after delivery make a human mother uniquely capable of loving and caring for her offspring. Obviously, a great deal is at stake if the mother's initial feelings and behaviours toward her newborn have long-term consequences for their future relationship. Human infants have to be protected and nurtured for a long time and whatever the lip-service paid to sexual equality and interchange of roles, it is the female (as in most mammalian species) who is the main care-giver to the young offspring.

It is difficult to imagine a more daunting prospect to hold before an expectant mother than the possibility that a fortuitous separation from her infant might put a blight on her motherly love, if it occurs when she is optimally receptive to processes which will bind her to it. And in the light of what we know about the workings of self-fulfilling prophecies and their disruptive consequences, one would be hard put to think of a theory that offers more 'hostages to fortune' for a mother with a sick or premature infant, than this view of mother-to-child attachment.

This supposedly ethological explanation of the formation of bonds suggests that they develop during a sensitive (if not critical) period; in addition, attachment behaviour is seen as species specific and relatively uninfluenced by the previous experience and state of the mother or her expectations and cultural values. The processes underlying these momentous events after birth are not precisely specified, but it is postulated that the hormonal condition of the mother soon after birth, may facilitate acceptance of her child, and that contact through all the sensory modes also elicits attachment behaviour in the mother.

Signs of attachment

A distinction is drawn in the literature between the behaviours by way of which the maternal bond is first developed and which also serve to give expression to the subsequent relationship (so-called 'attachment behaviours'), and the inferred *attitudes* and *relation-ship* that lie behind such actions. Here we are referring to the tie between the mother and child (the 'attachment' which is discriminating and specific) which binds her to him in space and over enduring periods of time.

Enthusiasm for the notion that the early elicitation of certain attachment behaviours was crucial in bond-formation, seemed to gain support from studies[3] which claimed that mothers who had a lesser or greater amount of contact with their babies in the period following birth, showed some differences in later maternal behaviour. Klaus and Kennell[4] are concerned that separation of mother and baby during the first three days after delivery has an adverse effect on the mother because she loses the intimate contact with her infant at a time when she is highly sensitive to it. Increased interaction during this period is postulated to facilitate good mothering. We shall be examining the evidence in the following chapter.

But first it is necessary to try to clarify this extraordinary concept of maternal bonding – extraordinary because of its far-reaching implications, and because it is surely unprecedented to explain the acquisition of any other complex constellation of behaviours and attitudes in a *mature* human being, in terms of imprinting. The idea of maternal bonding is deceptive because, on first acquaintance, it looks so simple and straightforward. Nothing could be further from the truth. Ethological investigations of maternal behaviour in animals, and studies by developmental psychologists, anthropologists and psychoanalysts of human mothering, have given rise to a somewhat bewildering plethora of definitions and explanations of maternal attachment.

Much of the thinking about maternal attachment has been influenced by, and confused with, research into attachment between the infant and mother. In this work *proximity seeking* has commonly been utilized to index attachment; not surprisingly it finds its way also into key measures of maternal attachment. Behaviours which imply close contact – such as smiling, face presentations, cuddling, fondling, kissing, vocalizing, and prolonged gazing – are taken as indices of bonding. As we shall see in Chapter 4, research workers have tended to focus specifically on the mother's behaviour (e.g. touching, fondling), recording the amount of time spent in such activities; and in doing so they have neglected the contribution of the other member of the dyad − the infant. To parody that old song 'It takes two to tango', it takes two to interact.

The baby's response to his world is much more than a simple reaction to his environment. He is actively engaged in attempts to organize and structure his world.[5] Parents are not the sole possessors of power and influence within the family.[6] What is being suggested is that interactional sequences of mother − child, child − mother behaviours are likely to provide a better measure of the parent − infant relationship than a one-sided account. The notion of a dialogue (or 'conversation') between two individuals has been used as an indicator of the quality of attachments and gives rises to a definition of 'good' relationships expressed in terms of the reciprocity of interactions between the partners.[7] Both mother and child are active concurrently, each for part of the time; the 'good' mother is *responsive* to her baby and continues to respond until he is satisfied; she also *initiates* activities.

According to Klaus and Kennell,[4] the intimate mother − infant contact in the post partum 'sensitive period' gives rise to a host of innate behaviours; in their own words, 'a cascade of reciprocal interactions begins between mother and baby (which) locks them together and mediates the further development of attachment'.

The idea of the female role

Bonding is often indexed by nurturant, care-giving behaviour − for example, the quality of the mother's feeding of her infant.[8] Again, the bonding metaphor makes something special, and specifically female, of this role. By now (if not a good deal earlier) readers are likely to be chaffing at the bit and saying to themselves: 'Why this preoccupation with mother love and maternal attachment? What about paternal love, the father's attachment to his offspring?' Pawson and Morris provide a medical opinion:[9]

Unlike women, they have no hormone changes, no remarkable physical and *emotional* experiences to help them adapt and identify with their new child. It is a secondary form of relationship.

At first glance, Klaus's description of *maternal bonding* (as a sex-linked attribute) seems plausible, and the practice of giving mothers freer access to their babies, progressive; indeed, many practitioners have adopted these ideas with conviction. Whatever else it is, maternal bonding makes for a compelling metaphor, evocative of mysterious and specifically female processes taking place during a relatively short period of time, which serve to 'bind' the mother to the child in a loving, enduring and caring relationship.

The psychoanalytic theorist, Erik Erikson, asserts that a woman's '. . . somatic design harbours an "inner space" destined to bear the offspring of chosen men, and with it, a biological, psychological, and ethical commitment to take care of human infancy'.[10] Not surprisingly women have protested at the biologically limiting message of such claims as Sigmund Freud's that the female's anatomy is her 'fate'.[11] The same restrictive element appears in the psychiatrist Joseph Rheingold's statement that 'woman is nurturance, anatomy decrees the life of a woman. . . . When women grow up without dread of their biological functions and without subversion by feminist doctrine, and therefore enter upon motherhood with a sense of fulfilment and altruistic sentiment, we shall attain the goal of a good life and a secure world in which to live it'.[12]

With the founder of psychoanalysis, and two eminent Harvard thinkers, lending their weight to popular stereotypes concerning the unique qualities of motherhood, we should (perhaps) not be surprised that the bonding idea has taken such a hold on the popular imagination. We have seen that it is possible to trace a continuity of child-care attitudes which have been steadily evolving to the recent preoccupation with bonding.

The cultural stereotype of motherhood is of something natural and instinctive. The concept of maternal bonding has the somewhat mystical overtones of maternal instinct and blood bond. One might argue that this is also apparent in what looks like an attempt to extend the symbiotic relationship of mother and offspring inherent in intra-uterine life, by prescribing a physical and psychological closeness between them for a substantial period of time after severing the umbilical cord. Perhaps an archetypal relationship like that between mother and child, and the kind of 'bonding contract' between them that is capable of lasting a lifetime, requires an explanatory theory (or metaphor) that matches it in dramatic impact. Add to these specifications the scientific respectability of the claim that maternal bonding is an imprinting-like phenomenon, and we have a concept that is well-nigh irresistable.

Sociologists are likely to reason that there is a more prosaic, indeed more sinister, explanation for the penetration of the public's consciousness by the bonding hypothesis. It is suggested that childhood is a social construction or invention. Far from being timeless, inevitable and 'natural', childhood emerged and evolved in particular historical circumstances in response to special social and economic changes. The same might be said of aspects of parenthood. Ideas about childhood − in the twentieth century most authoritatively stated by the disciplines of child psychology and psychiatry − often provide an underpinning for current social and economic practices by making them appear as natural, inevitable and therefore right.

It has been claimed that the maternal deprivation concept served to legitimize the social arrangement whereby mothers are expected to provide the predominant care for their offspring.[13] Is maternal bonding in this tradition? One would be hard put to find reference to *paternal* bonding. The father, in Western society, appears consistently in a role subsidiary to that of the mother − child relationship in the unfolding drama of the child's development.[14] Very little time and energy have been expended in discovering the psychological and sociological ramifications of fatherhood. We saw earlier his relationship with his child referred to rather dismissively as a 'secondary relationship'.

Richman and Goldthorp contrast such views with the dominance of the social stereotype of motherhood as being natural and 'the font of emotional support'.[14] Such ideologies (and they enjoy a long history) have, in their view, transformed pregnancy and birth into a female monopoly. They observe that developmental psychology has a close relationship with social policy and that it provides ideological reinforcement for the stereotype of motherhood. The father tends to be presented as being peripheral; he is accorded the status of genitor and external economic provider supporting the early mother − child bonding.

The relationship between ideas and social structure is a highly complex, speculative and polemical subject; it is not our task to explore it in detail here. However, it is as well to be aware of the way in which conventional theories of child-rearing appear to assume, or imply, that the contemporary nuclear family with its clear sex role divisions, and ascribed tasks, its emphasis on privacy and somewhat intense emotional attachments, is natural, unchangeable and functional for members of the family and society alike. These assumptions cannot be taken for granted. Paradoxically these same theories are pervaded by a preoccupation with the family's inadequacy and the mother's vulnerability when it comes to performing their 'natural' functions.

And it is precisely here that the male – female dichotomy is thought to have disadvantageous sexist connotations. When men are portrayed as economic providers, operating mainly outside the home to sustain the family unit, and mothers are presented as the providers of emotional support *within* the home, it is inevitable (if unjust) that mothers are most likely to be inculpated when the children develop problems. This sexist bias is buttressed intellectually by psychiatric theories and child-rearing philosophies.[15] Stella Chess, a child psychiatrist, refers to the phenomenon as '*mal de mere*' – the tendency to blame childhood psychopathology on mothers, who, at best, are incompetent, and at worse, cruel and neglectful. We return to this theme in Chapter 5.

The time of bonding

There is a wide spectrum of views about the nature and formation of bonds; they range from what might be called the 'unrestrained' perspective in which bonding is an imprinting-like phenomenon, brought forth given appropriate conditions during a critical sensitive (not merely sensitive) period, to the 'sanguine' view that relationships can be facilitated by encouraging their being practised during what is a foundational (significant, not critical) period in a mother's relationship. Klaus and Kennell, whose work is seminal in this field, seem to take a midway position.[4] They do not argue for a critical period, acknowledging that mothers can form attachments to their offspring after the first three days. Rather, they claim that the period is an optimal one for the development of a bond, and thus 'sensitive'.

We examine these issues in Chapter 4, and, in particular, the evidence for a sensitive period in the formation of bonds. Suffice it for the moment to acknowledge that there is ample evidence that much is at risk if a child is rejected over *long* periods of time by his care-givers, and they remain unresponsive to him/her.[1] For example, sensitivity to the infant's signals by his care-giver and the provision of a high level and variety of social stimulation in the first years of life fosters his development. These qualities in the inter-action between the baby and his care-giver in the early years appear to facilitate the development of a close attachment between the child and his mother in the child-to-parent direction. [16]

Cognitive development, even in the first 18 months of life, ap-pears to be influenced by the amount of variety of social stimula-tion provided, and the extent to which it synchronizes with the baby's needs. [17]

Vera Fahlberg, in her book in the popular '*Practice Series*' en-titled *Attachment and Separation* claims that direct bonding be-tween the mother and child begins during the very first moments of the child's life. [8] She puts it in these words:

When a newborn infant is held horizontally, he reflexively turns his head toward the person who is holding him. The mother is pleased when the in-fant looks at her. She tends to caress the child gently. All of this exploring is part of the claiming process. During this process the mother is con-sciously and unconsciously looking for ways to tell her child from others. Studies based on videotapes of mother and child interactions made during deliveries and post-partum hospital stays indicate that when the mother doesn't take an active part in this claiming process the family is at high risk for severe parent – child difficulties in future years.

Unfortunately, citations are not provided for these studies. It is even suggested that there is a disproportional number of child abuse incidents affecting premature and sick infants as compared with the normal population of children. [18] Early separation is blamed.

What defines maternal attachment?

Whatever the dilemma of the practitioner who has to weigh up the evidence concerning bonding in the light of its practical conse-quences, the scientist has the responsibility to adopt a detached, ob-jective view of the subject. The first hurdle is to specify what it is he is trying to investigate, so as to be able to measure it. Opinions dif-fer about what constitutes maternal attachment. Bonding certainly implies a special and focused relationship towards the mother's own offspring. But what is this quality of specialness? One criterion might be the mother's own report of her attitudes and feelings towards the infant. Indeed, interviews [19] and self-rating scales [20] have been used to this purpose. The mother is adjudged 'attached' to the infant if she consistently, over an extended period of time, reports that she loves her child, feels responsible for him and has a sense of their mutual belonging. Conversely, the markers for an absence of bonding might be maternal reports of detachment, indifference or hostility towards the baby, and of having a sense of the child being a 'stranger' or separate from her emotionally.

This is all very well, but the hard-headed researcher could be excused for asking himself about the reliability of such reports; after all, deeds speak louder than words. He might be more impressed by a mother's actions than her rhetoric. By this token, a mother would be considered to be 'bonded' to her infant if she looked after him well (being aware of his needs and responding to them), gave him considerable and considerate attention, and demonstrated her love for him in the form of 'fondling, kissing, cuddling, and prolonged gazing'.[3]

Mother-to-infant attachment is usually inferred, in the scientific literature on bonding, from *observations* of just such behaviours, and additionally smiling, vocalizing, touching and face presentations. The trouble with these indices is that they belong to a range of so-called 'infant-elicited social behaviours' which are not only displayed naturally by care-givers, almost at a level of unawareness, but also by many strangers. They tend to occur together in one 'co-ordinated package'.[21] The mother performs a facial display, while vocalizing, while gazing and within the framework of a discrete head movement coupled with a face presentation. The fact that most normal women have a predilection to indulge in these pleasant, indeed affectionate, rituals – to smile, touch and tickle *other* people's babies when they meet them – despite there being no question of their being bonded to them, tends to undermine their significance as indicators of attachment.

Whether they are indicative of bonding obviously depends to some degree upon the research worker's or practitioner's *interpretations* of observed behaviour. Most scientific studies concern themselves simply with the amount of physical contact with, and care of, the baby. It is by no means self-evident that these interactions have got anything to do with specific bonding. Mothers who feel little or no affection or sense of belonging towards their offspring have been known to care meticulously – some would say as a compensation for their attitudes of rejection, of which they are ashamed — for the child. Mothers who cherish their children have also been known to abuse them at times of despair and acute frustration. Certainly in the case of attachment behaviour on the part of children, studies have indicated that *intense* displays of attachment behaviour by children do not necessarily imply *deep* attachments.[16] Account must be taken of settings and circumstances in which the different modes of behaviour are observed.

It is obviously no easy task to get at the essence of this so-called 'maternal bond', let alone measure it. Our assumptions about what constitutes the outward and visible signs of 'good maternal attachment' is likely to bias what we see and select from a mass of observations. The problem of specification of maternal bonding is like the proverbial elephant: difficult to define, but we like to think that we know one when we see one. Inherent in this frivolous observation is a serious problem of reification which tends to give 'maternal attachment', misleadingly, the attributes of *unidimensionality*. Is there any evidence that nurturant care is really like that? Or is the bonding process made up of several facets or dimensions? Most of the clinical discussions of bonding fail to take into account the formidable methodological problems of measuring the phenomenon; they seldom go beyond the circular ('it is what it is') kind of definition when they refer to good or poor bonding. The bonding concept is thus in danger of being used as a pseudo-explanatory construct which does not really indicate precisely what it means. To put it unkindly, it becomes the kind of 'thought-stopper' which was sometimes the role of the 'maternal deprivation' concept in professional case-conference discussions.

There is a need to assess the significance and inter-relatedness of those component behaviours thought to be indices of bonding. The assumption underlying the unidimensional view of bonding — that the various strands (or dimensions) of the so-called 'bond' are highly correlated — is questionable. But much more than that is implied! Bonding is assumed to be *unidirectional*; it is made to sound like a mechanical thing — the working of a kind of affectional superglue which will only 'take' if applied at the appropriate time and in the appropriate manner. If successful the mother (and the emphasis, as we have seen, is exclusively on the mother in the unrestrained view of bonding) is 'tied' or 'stuck' figuratively to her offspring. This mechanical model seems to suggest an all-or-nothing phenomenon.

There is no evidence that caring is really like that; it seems more likely to involve several dimensions of nurturance; in other words, each of these somewhat diverse features of caring is a matter of degree, i.e. it is measurable along a continuum. Dunn and Richards set out in a longitudinal study of 77 mother – child pairs (from birth to five years) to see if a number of categories of behaviours that have been used as indices of affection did indeed intercorrelate.[22] Correlations between measures were not high and they were unable to demonstrate a unitary attribute reflecting 'warm' mothering. The analysis of early feeding interactions indicated that measures of maternal affectionate behaviour do not co-vary in any simple way. The different facets of maternal style are associated with different infant and delivery factors; success and coordination of the feed, for instance, are affected by labour and delivery variables; total sucking, for example, is correlated with differences in the infant's reactivity (latency to cry on removal of teat) and not with the measurement of affectionate style and contact. Touching the baby – often used as an index of maternal feeling – did not correlate with the other measures of maternal 'affection'. It was noteworthy in this study that the baby was a vital contributor to the early differences in mother – child interaction.

In the case of infant-to-mother attachment, Ainsworth recommends the use of multiple criteria to describe the way in which such behaviour is organized and manifested.[23] No less should be demanded for mother-to-child attachment. However, the specification of the behaviours describing bonding remains problematic. For the scientist there is no escaping the obligation of trying to operationalize complex concepts and of trying to measure them, no matter how imperfectly. Appropriate scales of aspects of attachment behaviour and/or attitudes are required. Ideally the scoring should be carried out by observers without any prior knowledge of the mother – child relationship. The investigator must resist the temptation to disregard overt signs of attachment when he/she has already formed the opinion that a particular mother is not genuinely attached to her baby; for in such circumstances it is easy to reject verbal assurances of love, as well as actions normally indicative of maternal bonding, as spurious. Clearly, there are not a few pitfalls in the attempt to assess maternal attachment in its various social contexts.

References

1   Herbert, M. (1974) *Emotional Problems of Development in Children* (London: Academic Press).
2   Vesterdal, J. (1976) 'Psychological mechanisms in child abusing parents'. In Cook, J.V. and Bowles, R.T. (eds) *Child Abuse: Commission and Ommission* (Toronto: Butterworth).
3   Klaus, M.H. Jerauld, R., Kreger, N., McAlpine, W., Steffa, M. and Kennell, J.H. (1972) 'Maternal attachment − importance of the first postpartum days' *New England Journal of Medicine*, **286**, 460 − 63.
4   Klaus, M.H. and Kennell, J.H. (1976) *Maternal − Infant Bonding* (St Louis: Mosby).
5   Herbert, M. (1980) 'Socialization for problem resistance'. In Feldman, P. and Orford, J. (eds) *Psychological Problems: The Social Context* (Chichester: Wiley).
6   Harper, L.V. (1975) 'The scope of offspring effects: from caregiver to culture', *Psychological Bulletin*, **82**, 784 − 801.
7   Bakeman, R. and Brown, J.V. (1977) 'Behavioural dialogues: an approach to the assessment of mother − infant interaction', *Child Development*, **48**, 195 − 203.
8   Fahlberg, V. (1981) *Attachment and Separation*. Practice Series 5 (London: British Agencies for Adoption and Fostering).
    Floyd L. (1981) 'A model for assisting high-risk families in neonatal nurturing', *Child Welfare*, **60**, 4.
9   Pawson, M. and Morris, N. (1972) 'The role of the father in pregnancy and labour'. In *Psychosomatic Medicine in Obstetrics and Gynaecology* (Basel: Karger).
10 Erikson, E. (1964) 'Inner and outer space: reflections on womanhood', *Daedalus*, **93**, 582 − 606.
11 Freud, S. (1937) 'Analysis terminable and interminable'. In *Freud's Collected Papers* Vol. 5 (London: Hogarth Press).
12 Rheingold, J. (1964) *The Fear of Being a Woman* (New York: Grune & Stratton).
13 Morgan, P. (1975) *Child Care: Sense and Fable* (London: Temple Smith).
14 Richman, J. and Goldthorp, W.O. (1978) 'Fatherhood: the social construction of pregnancy and birth'. In Kitzinger, S. and Davis, J.A. (eds) *The Place of Birth* (Oxford: Oxford University Press).
15 Chess, S. (1964) 'Mal de mère'. Editorial in the *American Journal of Orthopsychiatry*, **34**, 613 − 14.
16 Ainsworth, M.D. (1973) 'The development of infant − mother attachment'. In Caldwell, B.M. and Ricciuti, H.N. (eds) *Review of Child Development Research* (Chicago: University of Chicago Press).
17 Beckwith, L. (1971) 'Relationships between attributes of mothers and their infants' IQ Scores', *Child Development*, **42**, 1083 − 97.
18 Brimblecombe, F.S.W., Richards, M.P.M. and Robertson, N. (eds), (1978) *Separation and Special Care Baby Unit*. Clinics in Developmental Medicine (London: SIMP).

19 Robson, K.S. and Kumar, H.A. (1980) 'Delayed onset of maternal affection after childbirth', *British Journal of Psychiatry*, **136**, 347 – 53.

20 Parker, G., Tupling, H. and Brown, L.B. (1979) 'A parental bonding instrument', *British Journal of Medical Psychology*, **52** 1 – 10.

21 Stern, D. (1977) *The First Relationship: Infant and Mother* (London: Fontana/Open Books).

22 Dunn, J.B. and Richards, M.P.M. (1977) 'Observations on the developing relationship between mother and baby in the neonatal period'. In Schaffer, H.R. (ed.) *Studies in Mother – Infant Interaction* (Academic Press: London).

23 Ainsworth, M.D.S. (1969) 'Object relations, dependency and attachment: a theoretical review of the infant – mother relationship', *Child Development*, **40**, 969 – 1025.

4

Is there a sensitive period for the development of maternal bonding?

We have seen in the preceding chapter that there is a widespread view that the experiences of the mother after the child's birth may affect her bond or attachment to the infant. Where her initial responsiveness is disrupted by separation (to take one example) there is a risk − it is feared − of long-term adverse consequences for the mother-child relationship. These important issues have aroused scientific interest. Thus we can draw on some years of research into the determinants, both genetic and environmental, of the mother's attachment to her offspring in the case of infra-human mammals.[1]

The influence of ethology

With regard to the human species, the last decade has witnessed a growing interest in the possibility that the development of mother-to-infant attachment (indexed by specific actions which serve to indicate affection and focused concern for the infant) is influenced by biological factors. The mother needs to be, as it were, bonded to her infant; her affection for her infant is treated by some writers as something she has to acquire over a limited period of time after the child's birth.[2]

Reading the literature on mother-to-child attachment induces a sense of *déjà vu*. The various preoccupations with the unidimensionality of attachment behaviour, its biological basis, the existence of a sensitive or critical period for the formation of attachments, the dangers of separation of mother and infant, are all reminiscent of the conjectures relating to the maternal deprivation hypothesis.[3] John Bowlby whose views have been so influential (and, sadly, so often misunderstood or misrepresented) in the areas of attachment theory and maternal deprivation, emphasizes that the baby's signals of (*inter alia*) distress, elicit the mother's comforting response.⁴ The crying and maternal response are thought to have a biological function; they serve as constituents of a system of behaviour binding child and mother closely together. Bowlby stresses the way in which the behaviour that attaches mother and child resembles that of infra-human primates; he points to the survival value of systems that ensure close proximity and contact between infant and mother during the long period of immaturity of all the apes, and, indeed, humans. Bowlby sees the young baby's crying as one of five *in-built* signals (crying, smiling, sucking, following and clinging) which, given the appropriate reaction of the mother, ensure physical closeness. His notion of the sensitive mother assumes a neat fit between the needs of the baby and the performance of the mother. Not only is the baby's behaviour 'built-in', but the mother is seen as genetically programmed to respond to the signals. She is 'biologically attuned' as a member of her species to them. This maternal sensitivity is thought to be critical for the development of a stable and happy relationship.

Richards notes how Bowlby's ideas about *attachment* in human babies have been transposed to mothers, but moved back in time to a much earlier period in the transactions between infants and their mothers, and the process renamed *bonding*.⁵ In the course of this transposition many of Bowlby's caveats and strictures with regard to the evidence on mother – child separations, his revisions of theory concerning the nature of attachment, seem to be overlooked. A stark 'critical period' hypothesis is applied to mother-to-child attachments, most particularly in practice settings, as if it were analogous (although the opposite side of the coin) to infant-to-mother attachment formation.

Why have allegedly ethological theories proved so attractive in explaining a large and complex segment of adult experience – no less than 'mother love'? We raised this question in Chapter 3, and also Stern's apposite description of infant-elicited social behaviours.⁶

Stern observes that by comparison with most acceptable and appropriate social behaviours between one adult and another (one might except lovers) the repertoire of a mother's actions toward her own infant are quite unusual – in fact rather deviant. He states that 'they would be considered outrightly bizarre if performed towards anyone but an infant. . . . When so directed, however, they comprise an expected and normal special subset of human behaviours, a subset belonging to the large category of parental behaviours.' The infant-elicited 'social behaviours' involve the mother performing a facial display, while vocalizing, (often in high pitched sounds and 'baby-talk' words) while gazing and making certain head movements.

The question of why babies elicit these behaviours raises all the problematical issues of innateness versus learning. Stern comments that when we see a set of behaviours that is almost universally used by society, in a particular natural human situation, and one which has had thousands of generations of evolutionary history to fashion an adaptive purpose, one is tempted to speculate that its acquisition is built upon some biological, indeed innate, basis. In a sense it *'looks* that way'!

The literature on maternal bonding is permeated with explanations – some with ethological overtones – which have their roots in the mother's biology. We need to be cautious about accepting such explanations uncritically. Although the infant-elicited 'social behaviours' are manifested by most mothers, it is acknowledged that there is marked variability in these maternal repertoires. It is also recognized that these and other 'natural' actions can be disrupted in the mother by an overlay of learned responses or due to the omission of crucial experiences. Such an interference with her natural repertoire of responses is of great concern to practitioners. They see cases – fortunately rather rare – of parents who fail to become attached in any meaningful sense to their offspring and who may overtly reject them. The antecedents and consequences of such failures are poorly understood. Attachment theory has been applied to this clinically important area without the benefit of the substantial research which accumulated over the years with regard to the child's attachment to the mother. It is notable how the early speculations about infant-to-mother attachments have been modified, and the more extreme statements and stark predictions moderated, in the face of growing empirical evidence.[3] Although the other attachments, those of adults to children, have been less extensively investigated, this has not prevented the case of mother-to-infant bonding (or its failure) from attaining some of the clinical significance and emotive connotations which in the early days were associated with the infant-to-mother construct.[7]

Clearly, what is needed is empirical evidence obtained specifically from studies of mothers' relationships to their offspring. There are various issues to disentangle in the rather confusing literature in this field. There are the separate questions of the time over which bonding takes place (e.g. in infancy only or later in life) and the variables (e.g. physical contact) which facilitate the development of the attachment. Let us, therefore, examine such evidence as is available. The widespread belief in the rapid bonding of the human mother to her offspring is rooted, in large part, in studies of maternal behaviour in animals.

In infra-human mammals, as in human beings, maternal behaviour is not equally directed to all infants of the species, but, on the contrary, tends to focus on the mother's own infants or the mother's adopted infants. It has been said in support of the bonding doctrine that the sensitive post-partum period for mother-to-infant bonding is not a purely human phenomenon, that it occurs in other mammalian species, and that, therefore, it should be regarded as a widespread biological/ethological characteristic of animal/human behaviour. The so-called maternal imprinting in sheep and goats has been cited as evidence that mothers in some mammalian species rapidly form strong attachments to their own newly born young.[8]

The conclusions about sheep and goats are drawn, however, from some early studies which subsequently turned out to require reinterpretation. These early studies showed that newborn lambs and kids would be most readily accepted by their mothers, and the mothers would treat the young as their own, when contact between the mothers and their offspring was allowed to be established soon after the birth event. It is noteworthy, however, that it was also reported a few years later that ewes and she-goats did sometimes adopt infants which were not their own. This would occur whenever a few days' proximity of infant and adoptive mother was enforced.[9]

It was clear from the start that the recognition of the mother's own or adopted infant, lamb or kid, was mediated by the sense of smell, known as olfaction. Some early reports of maternal attachments in sheep and goats called these attachments maternal imprinting, implying that mothers could become rapidly imprinted, as it were, onto their young (in a manner somewhat similar to the so-called filial imprinting, whereby goslings, ducklings and chicks become readily attached to a mother-goose, a mother-duck or a mother-hen). Because ewes and she-goats recognize their infants by smell, maternal attachment in these species was also sometimes called olfactory imprinting. Later investigations led to the abandonment of the notion of maternal olfactory imprinting because, in the light of the experimental findings, such terms seemed inappropriate for describing maternal behaviour in sheep, goats and other such mammals.

Very briefly, these later findings were, first, that mother-to-infant attachments in the species in question developed less rapidly than originally thought; and there was no strictly critical period for the formation of mother-to-infant bonds. Second − and this is most important − it was found that, in goats at least, the acceptability of infants to mothers depended on the absence of alien smells, or 'labels', on the infant. It is the presence of such alien smells − in practice the smells of other female animals − that evoke rejection behaviour, butting away of infants, in post-partum she-goats.[10]

We have given quite deliberately only a very brief summary of the findings. There are two reasons for not dwelling on this topic to any extent. The first is that it has turned out that there is not much at all in the behaviour of sheep and goats that resembles the bonding view of human maternal attachment, certainly no rapid bonding during a short sensitive period through skin-to-skin contact. The second reason is that even if something like this were present in sheep and goats, it would have little relevance to human bonding. Although they are mammals like sheep and goats, human beings are very differently constructed and their behaviour patterns have evolved very differently from the behaviour patterns of ungulates. Had something like rapid post-partum maternal bonding been observed in other primates, for example in monkeys or apes, then this might have been of relevance to the consideration of maternal bonding in our own species. However, no-one has claimed that this sort of bonding has been actually observed in monkeys or apes. In fact, it is known that in some monkey species at any rate, separation for a time of infant from mother after birth does not result in a diminished interest of the female in her infant. Thus, it does not appear as if any animal behaviour studies are at present germane to the consideration of the bonding doctrine.

*The effects of mother – neonate contact: experimental
studies*

We have seen that the belief in the rapid 'bonding' of the mother to
her newborn infant cannot readily be based on an appeal to work
with animals. Although the advocacy of attaching or 'bonding'
mothers to their newborn infants nowadays is widespread, the
number of empirical studies of humans relevant to this notion is
quite small. The earliest reports that mothers who had differing
amounts of contact with their babies in the early period after birth
showed some differences in later maternal behaviour are inconclusive, since an examination of the data shows that the
similarities in the maternal behaviour of both categories of mothers
far outweigh the differences.[11]

The Klaus and Kennell team, working in Cleveland, compared
the behaviour of 28 mothers of full-term infants: one group had experienced in the days after birth only the routine contact with their
babies that is traditional in American hospitals, while in the other
(experimental) group, mothers were allowed extra contact in the
first three days. Klaus and his colleagues did detect some differences in mothering behaviour between women who had the extended contact as compared with those who did not.[12] At one
month after birth the early-contact mothers spent more time in eye
contact with their babies and fondled them more during feeding
than the others. The information that was then lacking concerned
differences between the two groups during subsequent months, and
therefore it remained uncertain whether lack of lasting 'bonding'
could be inferred from the behaviour of the 'non-contact' mothers.

In an attempt to study maternal behaviour over a longer period,
the research team followed up one year later the mothers in the
study just mentioned.[12] The mothers were on this occasion interviewed and observed in a number of different situations. As the in-
vestigators pointed out, one year after the child's birth the extra
contact mothers did appear to be more attentive to the infants and
more responsive to them during a physical examination of the infants.[12] Nevertheless, the findings show that the mother – infant
interaction of the two groups was not significantly different in four
other situations which were observed, including a free-play session.
At two years of age, five mothers and infants from each group were
randomly selected for follow-up investigation.[13]

The extra contact mothers used significantly more questions, adjectives, words per proposition, fewer commands and content words than did the control group. This study was also concerned with children's speech development, where it could not be inferred that retardation was due to the restriction of the post-partum mother – infant contact rather than to a host of other factors.

The other research group (Leifer and colleagues) compared the behaviour of mothers of full-term babies, and two groups of mothers of premature babies, those only allowed visual contact with the baby after his placement in the intensive care unit, as is customary, and an experimental group who were allowed to participate in care-taking as far as was practicable.[14] While mothers of the full-term babies did maintain more ventral contact between themselves and their babies, and did smile more at the infants than mothers of the prematures one month after the baby's discharge from hospital, no differences were found between mothers of the full-term and premature babies in many other attachment behaviours (holding, affectionate touching, looking at, talking to, laughing or singing to the baby) or the time devoted to interaction with the baby outside care-taking. The two groups of mothers of prematures showed no differences at all in maternal behaviour, although mothers in the group who had experienced most separation were still somewhat less confident about their care-taking skills.[15] Nothing significant emerged from this investigation that demonstrated unequivocally any lasting disruption of normal maternal behaviour in the 'separation' group.

Although the Klaus and Kennell research team claim to have demonstrated that extra mother – child contact (16 hours) early in the child's life (the first three days) can influence the maternal relationship for a year or more, and argue further for a maternal 'sensitive period' after birth, the hypotheses remain unsupported. Some of the requirements for making their case – random allocation of subjects to conditions and 'blind' ratings of the data – are present in their work. What weakens their generalization is the small sample, biased in terms of its ethnic and class constituents. And more problematic are the weak 'effects' and the possibility that the women knew they were being treated differently and that the preferential treatment (rather than the early contact) produced the outcome.

Some other studies which have been occasionally quoted as confirming the hypothesis of rapid bonding during an early sensitive period are equally inconclusive. They are clinical studies, involving even smaller numbers of mothers, which have never been published in research-reporting journals. What is clear is that when authors have claimed that mother-to-infant bonding occurred, or failed to occur, in the early hours and days after birth evidence was entirely inadequate.

In more recent times, findings were reported which seemed at first to lend support to the bonding hypothesis. Thus a Swedish research group (Carlsson and his co-researchers) reported that contact between mother and infant for up to two hours immediately after birth facilitated the mother's feeding activity four days later.[17] Whether the longer-term consequence of this is stronger mother-to-infant attachment remains entirely unproven. In addition, Hales and his colleagues found that Guatemalan mothers given skin-to-skin contact with their infants immediately after delivery displayed significantly more affectionate behaviours — particularly in the '*en face*' regard — at 36 hours than did control mothers.[18] The researchers consequently argue for the importance of physical contact between the mother and her newborn during, at the very least, its first 12 hours of life.

Their findings were not confirmed by another Scandinavian study conducted by de Chateau and Wiberg.[19] Their group of 22 primiparous (first-time) mothers was given 15 minutes extra skin-to-skin and suckling contact with their infants after delivery. They differed at 36 hours from a control group of primiparous and multiparous mothers receiving *routine* care on only four out of 35 measured variables. There were no significant differences in maternal affectionate behaviours. Although *en face* and encompassing behaviours tended to occur more often in extra-contact mothers, the trend was not significant. The primiparous mothers were followed up at three months and one year following the infants' birth. At one year the mothers who experienced extra contact held their infants in closer body contact and for lengthier portions of the observational period than did control mothers. Touching and caressing (unrelated to caregiving) were more frequently observed, and greater warmth noted, in the behaviour of the extra contact group. In addition there were differences in the duration of breastfeeding in the groups (extra-contact range: 21 to 365 days;

average: 175 days; controls range: 10 to 240 days; average: 108 days).

The researchers are of the opinion that the relatively short period of extra contact during the first hour after delivery is scarcely sufficient by itself to explain later differences in maternal infant behaviour. They speculate that the pairs may find the opportunity during the early period 'to exchange signals that may be important to the establishment of mother – infant synchrony. Consequently, the development of the mother – infant relationship may proceed more smoothly.'

The Carlsson team decided to investigate 50 mother – infant pairs in order to ascertain the effects of various amounts of contact between mother and child on the mother's later nursing behaviour.[20] They found that at six weeks after delivery the nursing behaviours of the extended-contact and limited-contact groups were indistinguishable. As the authors say, their results are 'somewhat surprising' in view of the previous reports by Klaus, Kennell and their associates of 'persistent changes in the interaction of the mother and child as a result of extended contact immediately after birth'. Other researchers have also reported that whereas mothers with extended body contact with their babies immediately after delivery showed more tactual contacts with their newborns when observed during the first week after parturition than mothers who had been exposed to ordinary hospital routine, this group difference could not be observed five weeks later.[21]

Svejda and her colleagues with painstaking attention to methodological and procedural controls tested the hypothesis that early and enhanced mother – infant contact facilitates maternal attachment behaviour.[22] They used a double-blind experimental design, random assignment of 30 mother-and-infant pairs to contact conditions and response indices appropriate to the attachment construct. Fifteen healthy primiparous mothers had the infants for one hour at delivery and 90 minutes at each feeding. Another 15 were kept to the usual hospital routine for newly delivered mothers: brief contact at delivery and 30 minutes at each feeding. In order to minimize a feeling of 'specialness' in extra-contact mothers, mothers who were not in the study but who shared a room with these mothers, had their infants longer at each feeding so that this apparent difference in contact time would be eliminated. No differences in maternal behaviour were obtained on 28 discrete response measures or on pooled sets of individual measures (affectionate, proximity-maintaining, caretaking and miscellaneous response-types).

Evaluation of the evidence

We posed the following question earlier on: Do particular experiences, notably physical contact, facilitate (and we might have added 'determine') the mother's attachment to her baby? What is the 'state of play' on this vexed issue? Can we summarize the evidence and make a judgement about the status of this bonding hypothesis? What we seem to have is a situation in which one of the few carefully controlled investigations in this area of research such as the one just described together with the recent Swedish studies, fail to lend reliable support to the bonding hypothesis. Although there are studies which seem to indicate differences in maternal behaviour contingent on extra contact following birth, they are modest in magnitude and constitute a small fraction of a mother's repertoire of behaviours.[23] There is also an absence of any *clear-cut* link between some of the maternal behaviours being observed (despite the faith put in their pertinence in the literature) and the bonding construct. Nevertheless, there are strong hints that there may be short-term and *general* advantages in giving mother and baby the opportunity to get familiar with each other, as happens in the rooming-in tradition.[24] All relationships have to have a beginning point and require a framework within which mutual awareness and familiarity can grow. What we are talking about is foundational learning; learning how to relate to (and love) a stranger, a baby; and this learning for some seems to come quickly but for others more slowly.[25] Where better to begin than at the very beginning, with the newborn child placed in its mother's arms? But is it necessarily a disaster if and when this cannot occur? The evidence suggests the answer 'No'! It seems to be the case that most of the differences in maternal behaviour, associated with early contact, fade away with the passage of time. There is no hard evidence that irreversible damage is done to the mother who missed out on these early contacts because of this factor alone. Given reasonably 'normal' life-conditions, there is no compelling reason why she should not develop that heightened sensitivity to her child which is taken to indicate her attachment to it.

What the research *does* tell us is that there is a host of other factors in addition to early contact which have a bearing on mother – child relationships. Among the factors which can influence the way a mother behaves and relates to her offspring are her own cultural and social background, her own experience of being parented, her personality, her previous experience with babies and her experiences during pregnancy and birth.[25] Also important are the sex and temperament of her baby. In general the mother's previous experience of having infants is a potent influence on her actions with a new baby. Multiparous women appear more efficient in managing their child than primiparous women, and are less likely to be influenced by outside disturbances. They respond more quickly to their babies' crying and are more likely, subsequently, to feed them. They are less likely than primiparae to feel an *initial* indifference to the newborn baby – a not uncommon but disconcerting experience for first-time mothers.

A few studies have indicated that the mother's attitudes, measured *before* the child's birth, can affect the mother – child interaction. Positive attitudes toward infants have been found to be related to maternal responsiveness to the baby's crying[26] and to his/her social behaviour in the early months of life.[27]

Mothers who are highly anxious during the pregnancy have also been evaluated as having a less satisfactory interaction with their babies at eight months than mothers who had been low in anxiety.[28] Another study conducted by Hubert found that whether the baby was intended or not was related to the decision on whether to breast-feed.[29] These findings suggest, then, that the mother's attitudes during, or even before, pregnancy, may have some consequences for the mother – child interaction. Breast-fed infants, it seems, are fed for longer periods than bottle-fed babies during the first ten days of life, they spend less time in the cot and cry more, all of which may have possible consequences for the subsequent mother – child interaction and the child's development.[30]

However, although maternal attitudes before the child's birth probably do have some effects that are measurable in the early months of the child's life these should not be over-emphasized. Attitudes do tend to change favourably during pregnancy, even when the baby is initially unwanted.[29] Also, it is not simply that maternal attitudes determine the mother's behaviour with her child. The actual experiences with the child may also lead to more positive attitudes later.[31] It is also possible for mothers who began with very positive attitudes to the child to react to his or her difficult temperament with resentment and even hatred.[32]

We should not forget that the mother – child relationship in the early years develops out of an interaction uniquely brought about by the contribution of the mother *and* the contribution of the infant.[33] The sex, 'look' and temperament of a baby may affect the manner in which the mother initially responds to it. It has been shown that the same mother's sensitivity to a child's needs and provision of stimulation for him may be quite different for different children.[34] It has been shown that there tends to be less maternal attending to female than male babies. Maternal visual attention is thought to be one index of maternal bonding to the infant. Blind babies may disrupt their mothers' responsiveness to them because of the absence of eye contact. The infant's contribution by no means consists only of his genetically determined characteristics. He may learn as he grows older how to coerce his parents to perform deeds 'against their will' and against their better judgement.[35]

The mother's background – social class and cultural – appears to be a significant factor in studies of the way she relates to her child.[36] It is difficult to draw conclusions about the influence (or lack of one) of early contact on maternal behaviour when investigations fail to control this variable. In the Klaus and Kennell investigations, and in others dealing with underprivileged mothers, effects tend to be discovered which do not manifest themselves so clearly in studies of middle-class families.[19]

Social class might be expected to affect the mother's behaviour with her child through its influence both on attitudes and life-style. Among the major class differences found are variations in verbal behaviour and these appear very early. When the child is three months old the difference may lie not so much in the frequency of the mother's vocalizations as in their use.[37] Findings indicate that middle-class mothers are likely to respond to infant vocalization with a vocalization of their own, while working class mothers are more likely to touch the infant in response. By the time the infant is ten months, middle-class mothers do appear to vocalize more frequently than working class mothers.[36] Working class infants have been found to be as likely or even more likely to vocalize spontaneously than middle-class infants, so it seems unlikely that the class differences in the behaviour of mothers can be attributed to initial infant differences.[36,37] Tulkin and Kagan suggest that a possible explanation for the class differences may be a belief by the working class mother that the child cannot communicate with others and that, anyway, she can do little to influence his development.

There are other factors to take into account. Jones and his colleagues found that while extra contact made no difference to subsequent mothering behaviour, the age of primiparous mothers did.[38] These researchers reported that 'mothers 19 years of age and older demonstrated significantly more maternal responsiveness towards their infants that did mothers 18 years and younger'. Robson and Kumar noted that 'maternal affection was more likely to be lacking after delivery, if the mother had had a forewater amniotomy and had, in addition, either experienced a painful and unpleasant labour or been given more than 126mg. of pethidine'.[39] This is, of course, not an unexpected finding. What is also not unexpected is that Robson and Kumar found that three months after giving birth 'a mother was more likely to express feelings of dislike or indifference towards her baby if she was clinically depressed at that time'.

Maternal behaviour during feeding is a popular index of bonding in the literature, and there is even a rating scale available so as to be able to infer and measure the mother's bonding and attachment behaviour during these care-giving episodes.[40] We need to remember that differences have been found between mothers of first and later-born infants in their behaviour during the feeding of the newborn baby (at two days) which appear to be independent of the method of feeding.[41] Mothers of first-borns, whether bottle or breast-fed, devoted a greater length of time to the feeding process, showed more changes of activity during feeding, were generally less effective in feeding and dominated the feeding process more than mothers of later-borns. This finding suggests perhaps that mothers of first-borns tend to be more stimulating but less responsive. There is, in fact, some evidence that mothers of first-borns, at least those who are breast-feeding, are less responsive to the baby's crying than mothers of second-borns.[42]

Mothers of first-borns do face considerable difficulties in present-day society. The relative isolation of many families means that girls may have had no contact at all with a baby before the birth of their own. Despite the attempts of ante-natal clinics to prepare women for the care of their infants many have little appreciation of the needs of a young baby. In these circumstances it may be difficult for the mother to establish the sensitive interaction with the child which appears to be of such importance for later development. Of course, the position generally improves after the first six weeks or so. It has been shown, for a sample of American mothers of first-borns that the mother displays considerably more affection for the infant and is socially more responsive to him/her when he/she is three months old rather than three weeks.[26] This, it is suggested, is largely due to the maturation of the infant, but also partly to the mother's increased confidence and increased familiarity with the baby. Nevertheless, it may be that difficulties of the initial period do sometimes have lasting effects on the mother – child interaction. This question needs further investigation. Hubert's work indicates, at a minimum, that the mother of the first-born child needs far more help and support in the first weeks after birth than is generally offered at present.[29]

We posed a second question earlier on: does bonding occur only during infancy, or can it occur later? The answer lies surely in the extensive use by society of adoption. This idea of making use of adoption seems somewhat paradoxical given the importance attached to bonding in the caring process. We return to this issue in Chapter 5.

References

1 Rheingold, H.L. (ed.) (1963) *Maternal Behavior in Mammals* (New York: Wiley).
  Gubernick, D.J. and Klopfer, P.H. (eds) (1981) *Parental Care in Mammals* (New York: Plenum).
2 Klaus, M.H. and Kennell, J.H. (1976) *Maternal – Infant Bonding*. (St Louis: Mosby)
3 Rutter, M. (1972) 'Parent – child separation: effects on the children', *Journal of Child Psychology and Psychiatry*, **6**, 71 – 83.
4 Bowlby, J. (1979) *The Making and Breaking of Affectional Bonds* (London: Tavistock)
5 Richards, M.P.M. (1979) Effects on development of medical intervention and the separation of newborns from their parents. In Shaffer, D. and Dunn, J. (eds) *The First Year of Life*. (Chichester: Wiley).
6 Stern, D. (1977) *The First Relationship: Infant and Mother* (London: Fontana/Open Books).

7 Valman, H.B. (1980) 'The first year of life: mother – infant bonding', *British Medical Journal*, **280**, 308 – 10.
   Sugarman, M. (1977) 'Paranatal influence on maternal – infant attachment', *American Journal of Orthopsychiatry*, **47**, 407 – 21.
   Klaus, M.H. and Kennell, J.H. (1976) 'Parent-to-infant attachment'. In Hull, E.D. (ed.) *Recent Advances in Paediatrics, Vol. 5* (Edinburgh: Churchill Livingstone).

8 Collias, N.E. (1956) 'The analysis of socialization of sheep and goats', *Ecology*, **37**, 228 – 39.
   Hersher, L., Richmond, J.B. and Moore, A.U. (1963) 'Modifiability of the critical period for the development of maternal behaviour in sheep and goats', *Behaviour*, **20**, 311 – 20.

9 Klopfer, P.H. (1971) 'Mother love: what turns it on', *American Scientist*, **59**, 404 – 7.
   Gubernick, D.J. (1980) 'Maternal "imprinting" or maternal "labelling" in goats?', *Animal Behaviour*, **28**, 124 – 9.

10 Gubernick, D.J. (1981) 'Mechanism of maternal "labelling" in goats', *Animal Behaviour*, **29**, 305 – 6.

11 Klaus, M.H., Jerauld, R. Kreger, N., McAlpine, W., Steffa, M. and Kennell, J.H. (1972) 'Maternal attachment – importance of the first postpartum days', *New England Journal of Medicine*, **286**, 460 – 3.

12 Kennell, J.H., Jerauld, R., Wolfe, H., Chester, D., Kreger, N., McAlpine, W., Steffa, M. and Klaus, M.H. (1974) 'Maternal behavior one year after early and extended postpartum contact', *Developmental Medicine and Child Neurology*, **16**, 172 – 9.

13. Ringler, N.M., Kennell, J.H., Jarvella, R., Novojosky, B. and Klaus, M.H. (1975) 'Mother-to-child' speech at two years – effects of early postnatal contact, *Journal of Pediatrics*, **86**, 141 – 4.

14 Leifer, A.D., Leiderman, P.H., Barnett, C.R. and Williams, J.A. (1972) 'Effect of mother – infant separation on maternal attachment behavior', *Child Development*, **43**, 1203 – 18.

15 Seashore, M.J., Leifer, A.D., Barnett, R. and Leiderman, P.H. (1973) 'The effects of denial of early mother – infant interaction on maternal self-confidence', *Journal of Personality and Social Psychology*, **26**, 3, 369 – 78.

16 Klaus, M.H. and Kennell, J.H. (1978) 'An early maternal sensitive period? A theoretical analysis', In Stern, L. (ed.) *Intensive Care in the Newborn, II.* (New York: Masson).

17 Carlsson, S.G., Fagenberg, H., Horneman, G., Hwang, C.P., Larsson, K., Rodholm, M., Schaller, J., Danielsson, B., and Gundewall, C. (1978) 'Effects of amount of contact between mother and child on the mother's nursing behaviour', *Developmental Psychobiology*, **11**, 143 – 50.

18 Hales, D.J., Lozoff, B., Susa, R., and Kennell, J.H. (1977) 'Defining the limits of the maternal sensitive period', *Developmental Medicine and Child Neurology*, **19**, 454 – 61.

19 De Chateau, P. and Wiberg, B. (1977) 'Long-term effect on mother – infant behavior of extra contact during the first hours postpartum:

follow-up at three months', *Acta Paediatrica Scandinavia*, **66**, 145 – 51.

20   Carlsson, S.G., Fagenberg, H., Horneman, G., Hwang, C.P., Larsson, K., Rodholm, M., Schaller, J., Danielsson, B. and Gundewall, C. (1979) 'Effects of various amounts of contact between mother and child on the mother's nursing behavior: a follow-up study', *Infant Behaviour and Development*, **2**, 209 – 14.

21   Schaller, J., Carlsson, S.G. and Larsson, K. (in press) 'Effect of extended postpartum mother – child contact on the mother's behavior during nursing', *Infant Behavior and Development*.

22   Svejda, M.J., Campos, J.J. and Emde, R.N. (1980) 'Mother – infant "bonding": failure to generalize', *Child Development*, **51**, 775 – 9.

23   MacFarlane, A. (1975) 'The first hours and the smile'. In Lewin, R. (ed.) *Child Alive* (London: Temple Smith).

24   O'Connor, S., Vietze, P.M., Sherrod, K.B., Sandler, H.M. and Altemerer, W.A. (1980) 'Reduced incidence of parenting inadequacy following rooming-in', *Paediatrics*, **66**, 176 – 82.
Greenberg, M. (1973) 'First mothers rooming-in with their newborn: Its impact on the mother', *American Journal of Orthopsychiatry*, **43**, 783 – 8.

25   Robson, K.M. (1981) 'A study of mothers' emotional reactions to their newborn babies'. Unpublished PhD thesis, University of London.

26   Moss, H.A. (1967) 'Sex, age and state as determinants of mother – infant interaction', *Merrill-Palmer Quarterly*, **13**, 19 – 36.

27   Moss, H.A. and Robson, K.S. (1968) 'Maternal influences in early social visual behaviour', *Child Development*, **39**, 401 – 8.

28   Davids, A., Holden, R.H. and Gray, G.B. (1963) 'Maternal anxiety during pregnancy and adequacy of mother and child adjustment eight months following childbirth', *Child Development*, **34**, 993 – 1002.

29   Hubert, J. (1974) 'Belief and reality: social factors in pregnancy and childbirth'. In Richards, M.P.M. (ed.) *The Integration of a Child Into a Social World* (Cambridge: Cambridge University Press).

30   Richards, M.P.M. and Bernal, J.F. (1971) 'Social interaction in the first days of life'. In Schaffer, H.R. (ed.) *The Origins of Human Social Relations* (London: Academic Press).

31   Herbert, M. (1978) *Conduct Disorders of Childhood and Adolescence: A Behavioural Approach to Assessment and Treatment* (Chichester, John Wiley.)

32   Herbert, M. and Iwaniec, D. (1977) 'Children who are hard to love', *New Society*, **4**, 21 April, 111 – 12.

33   Korner, A.F. (1974) 'The effect of the infant's state, level of arousal, sex and ontogenetic stage of the caregiver'. In Lewis, M. and Rosenblum, L.A. (eds) *The Effect of the Infant on its Caregiver* (New York: Wiley).
Lewis, M. and Lee-Painter, S. (1974) 'An interactional approach to the mother – infant dyad'. In Lewis, M. and Rosenblum, L.A. (eds) *The Effect of the Infant on its Caregiver* (New York: Wiley).

34 Lewis, M. (1972) 'State as an infant – environment interaction: an analysis of mother – infant interaction as a function of sex', *Merrill-Palmer Quarterly*, **18**, 95 – 122.
Schaffer, H.R. (1977) *Mothering* (London: Open Books/Fontana).
Yarrow, L.J. (1963) 'Research in dimensions of early maternal care', *Merrill-Palmer Quarterly*, **9**, 101 – 14.
35 Bell, R.Q. (1972) 'Stimulus control of parent or caretaker behaviour by offspring', *Developmental Psychology*, **4**, 33 – 72.
36 Tulkin, S.R. and Kagan, J. (1972) 'Mother – child interaction in the first year of life', *Child Development*, **43**, 31 – 41.
37 Lewis, M. and Wilson, C.D. (1972) 'Infant development in lower-class American families', *Human Development*, **15**, 112 – 17.
38 Jones, F.A., Green, V., and Krauss, D.R. (1980) 'Maternal responsiveness of primaperous mothers during the postpartum period: age differences', *Paediatrica*, **65**, 579 – 84.
39 Robson, K.M. and Kumar, R. (1980) 'Delayed onset of maternal affection after childbirth', *British Journal of Psychiatry*, **136**, 347 – 53.
40 Floyd, L. (1981) 'A model for assisting high-risk families in neonatal nurturing, *Child Welfare*, **LX** (9).
41 Thoman, E.B. Leiderman, P.H. and Olson, J.P. (1972) 'Neonate mothers interaction during breast-feeding', *Developmental Psychology*, **6**, 110 – 18.
42 Bernal, J. (1972) 'Crying during the first ten days of life and maternal responses', *Developmental Medicine and Child Neurology*, **14**, 362 – 72.

5

Practical consequences of the bonding doctrine

The issues raised by the bonding doctrine are not solely academic. The impact of the doctrine upon the thinking of practitioners in obstetric and paediatric fields has been considerable. It has markedly influenced the procedures adopted by nurses, and especially by midwives and health visitors, and the types of advice they give to their patients and clients. The doctrine has also impressed itself in the field of social work, particularly in relation to child abuse, but also throughout the whole area of child welfare. In this chapter we shall deal with the bonding doctrine as it affects procedures followed by those concerned with the care of newborn infants, including premature, physically handicapped and mentally handicapped ones, failure-to-thrive children and autistic children; we shall also consider, in the light of the bonding doctrine, problems of maternal rejection, adoption and fostering, and especially child abuse.

Maternal attachment to full-term infants

In view of what has been said in previous chapters, there is little else that needs additionally to be considered at this stage. It goes without saying that it is in the interest of both the mother and her baby that they should stay together after birth. The umbilical cord no longer literally links them together, but, metaphorically speaking, the tie persists in that skin-to-skin contact provides for mutual comfort. Such contact, however, is not a *sine qua non* of happiness or of successful growth of mutual attachment. Certainly mother-to-infant attachment can develop, and normally does develop, irrespective of any direct or prolonged contact in the hours or days immediately following birth. The mechanisms of the development of maternal attachment, the factors in the environment, and within

48

the mother and the infant, which are either conducive to, or hinder, a vigorous growth of parental bonds — these are matters to be considered at length in Chapter 6.

Bonding after a caesarian section

A caesarian section is only performed if something has gone wrong for either the mother or the baby or both. As is well known, it is the delivery of a baby through a cut made into the abdominal wall instead of the normal delivery through the vagina. Some mothers can only have babies if a caesarian section is performed. With others the caesarian is a last minute 'crisis' decision to save the mother's or, more often, the baby's life. Premature babies are often delivered by caesarian section because this is less of a risk to a baby already under some degree of stress. If the afterbirth is in front of a baby, a condition known as *placenta praevia*, a caesarian section is also performed as soon as possible.

In the past mothers were always given a general anaesthesia for a caesarian as a matter of routine, which meant that the mothers were unconscious right through the birth of the baby and for some time afterwards. However, nowadays some mothers who need to have a caesarian section choose to have their babies delivered with the help of an epidural injection. This is an injection into the space between the vertebrae at the base of the spine which numbs all (or most) sensation from the waist downwards. Thus the mother is fully conscious when her baby is taken out of the womb. This has some advantages and also allows the father to share with the mother in the moment of birth. In this way a birth by caesarian section can retain some of the features of a normal confinement.

Those who believe that for bonding to occur there must be skin-to-skin contact immediately after birth have always felt concern over the effects of a caesarian birth on the mother – child relationship. They may worry less when the mother remains conscious following an epidural injection, as she is able to hold her baby as soon as it is delivered. But what are the facts of the situation?

A caesarian section, often preceded by a crisis, transforms a birth-event into a major abdominal operation from which the mother needs time to recover physically and mentally. There is no evidence at all that these mothers are ultimately less attached to their babies. It is just that immediately after the operation they may be too dazed to be as interested in their babies as are mothers after normal confinements. As Welburn says when referring to caesarian births, 'no mother should be forced through a ritual bonding period if she isn't initially interested in her baby'.[1] It may seem far-fetched but one can well imagine a situation in which mother-and-baby bonding becomes a time-tabled hospital procedure — the clinical *reductio ad absurdum* of a compelling but unproven theory!

Maternal attachment to premature infants

The more serious question to which we must address ourselves is to what extent maternal attachment may be affected by the peculiar circumstances of the post-natal care of prematurely born babies. Such babies, after all, are fairly common. Low birth-weight and pre-term infants are typically placed in a special care nursery. This increases the chances that the mother and infant do not have much opportunity to interact in the early days following birth. How does this affect the mothers' feelings towards their babies, both in the short term and in the longer term? Disquiet about separation has been voiced by some (often middle-class) parents and by many professionals such as paediatricians, medical social workers and psychologists.

To begin with, premature birth can be a somewhat traumatic experience for the mother. The low weight of the baby can itself be worrying. A mother who smoked during pregnancy may be concerned with some justification lest she herself is to blame for the baby's low birth-weight. Thus at the time her anxiety may be due as much to these and related factors as to the enforced separation from her baby. Whatever feelings she harbours towards her baby are clearly the result of a complex set of events and experiences, and certainly are not solely the result of a lack of skin-to-skin contact.[2] If all goes well with the infant in the special care unit, and the parents can clearly observe this in the course of frequent visits, then, their anxiety is likely to be allayed. There is no evidence that in such circumstances parental love and attachment will be in any way diminished.

To be discharged from hospital and to return home without her baby is a situation fraught with difficulty for any mother. It is a situation which is contrary to the expectations of her friends and neighbours: a good deal of explaining has to be done, which may or may not be somewhat distressful or tiresome. In the end, sooner or later, the baby is returned to the mother: and there is no evidence that the mother's feelings towards her infant are in any way permanently distorted. Of course, parental access to their babies in special care units is to be greatly encouraged for a variety of good reasons: but practical common sense, rather than concern over the existence of a critical bonding period, should decide upon visiting arrangements.

Those are the conclusions that can be reasonably drawn from the present state of knowledge. However, that is not to say that our knowledge in this field is adequate or satisfactory. As one group of authors say, the present 'scientific' evidence on the adverse effects of parent – child separation in the immediate neonatal period is partial and incomplete.[3] There is, however, a good deal of evidence that babies can weather prolonged early parental separation and thrive in every way thereafter.[4] There are also numerous indications that mothers can in favourable circumstances function perfectly well after being reunited with their premature babies, care for them competently, and become attached to them as strongly as do mothers of full-term babies.

Maternal attachment to physically and mentally handicapped infants

Depending on the nature and severity of the handicap, a firm diagnosis may be possible at any time, ranging from birth onwards. If the mother is initially unaware of the infant's disability, then clearly the development of maternal attachment remains unaffected until the time she learns about it. And even then, whatever the child's age, her feelings about the child may remain substantially unaltered one way or another. If the mother learns about her baby's handicap at birth, she is, of course, likely to be markedly affected by the news. The question is whether her love for the baby then develops normally or abnormally; and if the latter we may ask whether her bond of affection is weaker, stronger or different in quality from what it might otherwise have been.

The clearest diagnosable type of handicap at birth is a congenital abnormality of structure. According to the Department of Health statistics, there are up to 40 such babies born each day in Britain, and the survival rate is increasing all the time. How do mothers and the rest of the family react to the birth of such infants? One systematic small-scale study was carried out more than a decade ago in the hope of finding an answer.[5] Not at all surprisingly, the initial emotional reaction of the mother was found to be anxiety, shock or dismay in facing an unexpected crisis. This overshadowed the satisfaction normally accompanying child-birth. After a time interval, some mothers tended to play down the problem, and early mothering care seemed essentially unaffected. Studies like this are very useful in suggesting how the situation can best be managed by doctors, nurses and social workers. It is very difficult, however, to assess what the impact of the birth of a handicapped infant is on the development of the mother-to-infant bond.

When asked, most mothers express the view that it is best for them to be told as soon as the doctor suspects a physical or a mental defect in the infant.[6] They wish to be given this information, but some mothers adopt what looks like a defensive stance and deny the diagnosis. They certainly often continue to hope that the doctor will be proved wrong. Such denial is not uncommon immediately following diagnosis and goes on for some days or weeks, or even longer, before it finally abates.[7] The doctor has to decide how soon he or she is in a position to tell the parents of their infant's disability; also how much to tell them. For one thing, sometimes young mothers are so overwhelmed by the initial news that they cannot take in much more than the barest outlines of the situation. Finally, the problem faced by the doctor is not only when and what to tell the mother but also what not to tell her. It is often a question of not giving the parents information which could be misinterpreted and sparing them any further unnecessary suffering.[6]

We are conscious of not having stated in an unequivocal manner whether there is anything different and special about maternal attachment to physically and mentally handicapped infants. There are reports of resentful and rejecting mothers; equally, some mothers are exceptionally loving and devoted to their handicapped children. In many cases, initially, babies other than perfectly normal seem unacceptable. But, remarkably, mothers and fathers come to accept the unacceptable.[8] Much learning is involved in this; and learning in a broad sense applies not only to knowledge and skills but also to feelings and motives. As we shall see in the next chapter, one may credibly view attachment to a large extent as the result of 'exposure learning', as something that 'grows on one'.[9] Although the shock of becoming a parent of a child with a disability can make a difference to the character of the parent – infant relationship, there is no reason to view maternal bonds to a child, handicapped or otherwise, as other than an attachment of one human being to another. It is perhaps worth bearing in mind that attachments of one individual to another can also cross the species boundaries. There is something in the dog's tie to his master that strongly resembles the master's attachment to his dog.

Bonding and disturbed mother – child relationships

The concept of maternal bonding, i.e. rapid mother-to-infant attachment, appears frequently in professional discussions of childhood psychopathology and child neglect. 'Bonding' is used as a diagnostic concept, and one which has to bear the weight of important explanatory, descriptive and predictive statements. Failures or deficiencies of the maternal bond are blamed for incidents of child rejection and cruelty. Such failures are related aetiologically to the quantity and quality of post-partum contact between mother and infant. Thus it is asserted that the separation of the mother and neonate for several days or weeks – in the event of prematurity or illness requiring intensive care – may damage irreversibly the subsequent mother – child relationship. Such an eventuality puts the child at risk in a variety of ways, notably in developing psychological disorders, failing to thrive or becoming a victim of abusive treatment.

The blame for much of the psychopathology of childhood has been put fairly and squarely – indeed, not so fairly – on the shoulders of women. The social work and child psychiatric literature over many years has been replete with 'pathological mothers', schizophrenogenic mothers, asthmagenic mothers, mothers accused of freezing out their autistic children by the cold intellectualization of their maternal role, or suffocating their allergic offspring with the warmth and overprotectiveness of their attachment to them. Our society tends (when things go wrong) to inculpate mainly the noxious attitudes of the female in her child's problems; she rejects, overprotects, punishes or double-binds him into abnormality.

The particular concern with the consequences of maternal loss and rejection as the mediators of various forms of deprivation — notably love and stimulation — has had far-reaching practical implications. There has been an increased sensitivity (some might say hypersensitivity) to the vital environmental facilitators of healthy infant development in hospital wards, day-care settings and remedial centres for physically and mentally handicapped children. But much practice (and research) is based on a unidirectional model which emphasizes mother-to-infant influences, particularly the negative ones. This reflex tendency to scapegoat mothers has also entered the paediatric literature. Foolish or reprehensible child-rearing practices on the part of the mother and distortions in the formation of her attachments to her offspring are held responsible for deleterious effects upon the child's psychological and physical well-being. As Chess explains:[10]

The standard procedure is to assume that the child's problem is reactive to maternal handling in a one-to-one relationship. Having come to this conclusion, the diagnostician turns her further investigations unidirectionally toward negative maternal attitudes and the conflicts presumed to underlie these. Investigation in other directions is done in a most cursory fashion or not at all. At the diagnostic conference, speculations are made concerning the mother's relationship with her own parents, and her over-compensation for the rejection. Single bits of data fitting in with the speculations are quoted as typical of the child's feelings and the mother's attitudes are taken as proof of the thesis of noxious maternal attitudes as universal causation.

An interesting example of the explanation of a serious clinical phenomenon in terms of maternal rejection is seen in the syndrome known as infantile autism.

Maternal bonding and infantile autism

The symptoms of the disorder called early infantile autism are not clearly in evidence until the child is about a year old. Such a child shows undue passivity and lack of interest in the events around it. Unlike a normal child, it does not appear to treat its mother as a very special person. Later on, it is unable to form normal social relationships. Its language development is very markedly retarded. Although in many ways autistic children initially appear to be no less intelligent than their peers, they tend to exhibit a variety of peculiar mannerisms and obsessions. Later, a large percentage function at a severely subnormal level, though still showing 'islets of intelligence'. Such, in the broadest outline, is the clinical picture of autistic children, first described in the early 1940s in America by Leo Kanner.[11] It is noteworthy that Kanner referred to the condition as one of 'extreme aloneness' and asserted that by this he did not mean that the child showed 'withdrawal'. This is of significance not only in characterizing the syndrome but also in regard to its aetiology.

Theorising about childhood autism soon began to develop along the traditional American environmentalist lines. Environmentalism is a common feature of Freudian, psychodynamic thinking and of behaviourism, both stressing the influence of early experience in moulding the individual's personality. More specifically, Bettelheim expressed the view that the autistic condition was caused by the mother's unconscious rejection of her child from the very beginning.[12] The notion gradually gained ground that 'bonding failure' on the part of the mother was at the root of childhood autism. This, incidentally, had never been claimed by Kanner himself, who had earlier described and named the syndrome.

Undoubtedly, the bonding-failure theory had some plausibility. It explained the autistic child's 'aloneness' as a retreat to a world of his own in response to the mother's lack of genuine affection. The child's strange modes of behaviour were thought to be defences against anxiety generated by living in an essentially unfriendly environment. As a result of this view, in many cases mothers of autistic children were given 'appropriate' psychotherapy. The unhappy impact of such treatment is vividly described by one mother who had been a recipient of it.[13] She found the insinuation that autism is caused by parental rejection to be unfounded and unhelpful in dealing with problems she was facing. What evidence, then, was there for this alleged maternal rejection, and especially for the absence of maternal attachment from birth onwards?

When evidence began to be sought systematically, none was forthcoming. Most of the brothers and sisters of autistic children are not in the least autistic themselves; if it is the mother, or the parents, who are responsible, why are some of their offspring autistic and the majority not? One comparative study of parents set out to devise measures to assess parental characteristics generating infantile autism. Then, using these measures, it was found that there were no differences between parents of control group children and autistic children with regard to 'parental warmth, emotional

demonstrativeness, responsiveness, or sociability, parental psychiatric disorder, or with respect to early stresses of any kind'. It was
concluded that it is unlikely that autism develops as a consequence
of how the parents behave and certainly not as a result of their personality attributes.[14] Parental behaviour can, of course, be affected by the autistic behaviour of their child; but the former is the
consequence of the latter rather than its cause. All this does not
mean that nothing can be done by way of manipulating the environment to alleviate the autistic condition. Foremost amongst the
many researchers concerned with both defining the condition more
clearly and, especially, finding ways and means of alleviating it has
been Lorna Wing.[15] More recently, further promising approaches
to the treatment of infantile autism have been explored by the
Tinbergens; but they are concerned much more with obstacles to
the formation of infant-to-adult attachments than mother-to-
infant bonding.[16]

The bonding doctrine and failure-to-thrive infants

It has been claimed, suggested or implied that the lack of maternal
attachment, or inadequate attachment, is responsible for a variety
of other conditions affecting children; these include child abuse by
the mother, and even defective weight gain and growth retardation
in infants. It has long been known that some babies and even older
children may fail to put on weight in accordance with accepted
guidelines for growth, when their caretakers are hostile. In the past
'not thriving' was known as marasmus, and its cause was
unknown.

More recently, since the effects of maternal deprivation have
been more closely studied, what has been described as the
'nonorganic failure to thrive' syndrome has puzzled paediatricians,
child psychiatrists, psychologists and neurologists, because these
children's inability to grow is not necessarily due to insufficient
food-intake. Indeed some of them have compulsive eating habits.
Nor can the disorder be traced to any physical condition. Test feeds
may show the mother's milk supply to be satisfactory. A thorough
search for infections may show negative results. Many, however,
do have severe feeding problems when given food by their mothers.
It has therefore been proposed that the condition has to do with a
faulty mother-to-infant relationship, and more specifically, the

mother's psychological make-up, comparable to that which underlies the battered child syndrome to be considered later in this chapter.[17] It is said that the mother fails to provide an appropriately nurturing environment in which her infant can develop normally. How such maternal neglect has its *precise* effects is not identified in the research literature. But lack of true attachment of the mother to her infant in the neonatal period is seen as an underlying factor.[18] A highly speculative hypothesis has been put forward that neglect affects growth through a physiological pathway in the neuro-endocrine system, but so far no conclusive evidence has been found. Further, it has been suggested that in an emotionally deprived environment abnormal patterns of sleep inhibit the secretion of pituitary hormones, including the growth hormones.[19]

Whatever the exact cause, and none has been found as yet, there is little doubt that we have here a disturbance of the mother – child relationship, though it is a moot point whether it is a cause or effect of the children's failure to thrive. Pollitt *et al.* have described the maternal behaviour of these mothers as 'inoperant' because they have been observed in numerous situations to behave less effectively than mothers of thriving children.[20] But the lack of interaction and other abnormal 'relatedness' may be as much due to a temperamental mismatch between mother and child as to some pathology in the mother arising from a stressful childhood.

An unusually large-scale study of 1,400 women allowed the researchers to examine precursors of failure to thrive that were obtained prior to diagnosis.[21] In order to eliminate some of the sources of error in understanding the multiple factors related to child maltreatment in general, a prospective longitudinal design was used in which this large cohort of women was interviewed during the first trimester of pregnancy. The authors used an interview, developed to identify families most likely to contain an infant later identified as maltreated. About a third of the women and their infants were followed up until the infants were 18 months of age. After the infant's first two weeks, a sub-sample of these mother – infant dyads were diagnosed as having nonorganic failure-to-thrive infants. The authors compared these dyads (35 in all) with normally growing infants and their mothers. Comparisons were made of multiple factors which included initial stable characteristics of mother and infant as well as measures of mother – infant interaction. No significant differences were found between mothers whose infants were later diagnosed as 'nonorganic failure-to-thrive' and those in the comparison group in which the children were growing adequately, with regard to their age, number of years in school, number of previous children, race, or marital status. In addition, there were no significant differences found for the results of the Maternal Attitude Scales, Maternal History Interview, Knowledge of Developmental Norms, or Life Stress Events. The fact that individual factors that comprised the interview did not show significant differences points to the importance of *multivariate analyses* – the analysis of several rather than single causal variables. The authors comment that the finding that the mothers who have infants with growth failure do not seem to differ along a number of dimensions from their peers with non-diagnosed infants, suggests that perhaps the differences in birth condition set up a chain of events resulting in poorly growing infants. A significant number were early birth or low birth-weight babies. The authors do not use this finding to invoke a simplistic explanation in terms of early separation or bonding failure, but insist on construing 'outcomes as having multiple historical and causal determinants, rather than single factor causes'. They formulate a complex train of events involving interactions between mother, child and other variables, with upsetting events like prematurity having an idiosyncratic effect depending upon the family in which it occurs.

Iwaniec and Herbert reported on a controlled study of 17 failure-to-thrive children and their mothers, using two contrast groups of hospitalized children.[22] They also describe in detail the treatment which centred on the family and aimed (*inter alia*) at improving feeding styles and modifying maternal behaviour in such a way as to make it more positive and enjoyable for both mother and child, and to increase frequency of interaction. Further they tried to help the mother to become more effective in controlling her child. This research (like the previous study) indicates that failure-to-thrive is a complex condition with varied antecedents affecting both mother and child which develops over a lengthy period. A significant proportion of the failure-to-thrive children had difficult temperaments from birth.

It was suggested earlier in the book that bonding, as the bedrock in the formation of the mother's attitudes towards and relationship with, her child, provides us with a particularly potent metaphor to exlain both significant phenomena (such as mother love) and certain distressing facts (like maternal cruelty). The trouble with metaphors, no matter how illuminating, is their tendency to inhibit precise analysis. Because of both its complexity and a lack of supportive evidence, the syndrome of failure-to-thrive cannot simply be ascribed to bonding failure *per se*, nor to relationship difficulties stemming from events occurring within a short period after birth. Indeed, if one did so, one might jeopardize treatment; in the study described above, a *broadly* conceived psycho-social therapeutic programme, mainly behavioural in orientation, achieved an 82 per cent success rate.

Bonding failure and child abuse

It is not uncommon at professional case conferences to hear a tragic case of child battering explained in terms of a failure, absence, or distortion of the mother's attachment to her infant. Child abuse – emotional and physical – is linked causally with a failure on the part of the mother to become 'bonded' to her child;[23] this in turn is traced to the early separation of mother and child.[24] It is claimed, for example, that there is an association among low birth-weight and pre-term infants and child abuse.[25] This, as we have seen before, is explained in terms of the removal of the baby from the mother while the infant is in a special (intensive) care unit.

The eminent paediatrician Hugh Jolly, writing in *Nursing Mirror* has this to say:[26]

Animal studies of the effects of short periods of separation of mother and offspring have shown disastrous consequences – rejection and even killing the baby. It is the realization that similar feelings can be experienced by human mothers when a baby has to be separated because of the need for special care that has led to great emphasis to ensure that the mother visits and touches her baby as often as possible, even if he is in an incubator and on a ventilator.

This kind of statement seems to reflect, in its concern with the risks of early separation, the influence of the 'ethological' model favoured by Klaus and Kennell[24] and, in the weight it gives to body-contact, the work of Harlow.[27] Such concern with the future well-being of mother and child on the part of practitioners is understandable and wholly admirable. However, we have the obligation to continue examining the evidence, as it is accumulating. To start with, what of this claim that mothers prone to baby battering are mothers who have not been bonded to their babies soon after delivery?[28]

Margaret Lynch and her colleagues concluded a retrospective study of 50 referrals to the Park Hospital service for child abuse in Oxford with the statement that 'at least 3 per cent of all mothers delivered at a large modern maternity hospital have identifiable problems likely to lead to a bonding failure or child abuse'.[28] The abused group were more likely to have been in the Special Care Nursery (59 per cent) than children from a contrast group referred to the maternity hospital social work department over the same period of time as the child abuse cases (24 per cent). Another investigation found that 24 per cent of abused children in a sample of 134 had been premature − four times the national average.[18]

What are we to make of these disturbing findings? It goes without saying that no-one can afford to be complacent in the face of this kind of evidence. And there is no comfort for the practitioner who reads the following kind of warning in a learned social work journal:[29]

Evidence for the absence, weakness or distortion of the usual affectional bond between parent and child, can be found in virtually every case of child abuse. . . .

Understandably the hard-pressed social worker cannot afford to be as complacent as the scientist in risking what the statisticians call 'Type II errors' − i.e. denying relationships which actually exist − because of a cautious attitude to evidence. Whilst it may be understandable that he or she errs on the side of making 'Type I errors' (asserting relationships falsely) in a fraught area like child abuse, the implications of Type I errors may also be harmful to clients. Interventions which, at best, are ineffectual, at worst demoralizing, may be the cost. In any event there *are* several problems connected with the findings described above. It is always difficult to be sure about the validity of retrospective information obtained from mothers about their pregnancy, the child's birth, the neonatal period and the youngster's early development. Granted that some studies rely on clinical records (perhaps more reliable than parental reports, although also at times somewhat suspect), far too much data is drawn from retrospective research designs to allow for confidence. Research samples also tend to be relatively small in number.

Where we do possess data from a relatively large scale investigation − a study of 240 mothers drawn from known-abuse, neglect and normal control populations − 'the hypothesized relationship between mother − neonate bonding and maltreatment was not supported'.[30] The multivariate analysis included 12 variables, of which six discriminated the abusing, neglecting and normal mothers at a high level of significance. Infant risk, determined on the basis of neonatal complications requiring hospitalization, was not a successful discriminator.

Vietze and his colleagues make the point that their findings of no differences in a wide variety of characteristics in the mothers of children maltreated in a way that affects their growth, and those whose children do thrive, 'contradict the assumptions and findings in the literature relating deviant maternal attributes to subsequent nonorganic failure-to-thrive'.[21] They note that 'the fact that this study was prospective rather than retrospective may be one way of accounting for the conflict in findings. The infants had not been identified at the time the data were being collected, and, thus, the mothers were not subject to the search for pathology which might occur once the diagnosis of growth failure was made.'

Even if we can accept the reliability of a positive association between child abuse and post-partum separations such as those occasioned by intensive care of premature infants, a correlation does not necessarily imply a causal relationship between the two variables. It could well be that they are associated with some third, underlying factor − say socio-economic class − and, in that sense, are not related to one another in a linear cause-effect manner.

Another group of researchers carried out a study of 32 separate low-birthweight babies and 32 controls specifically aimed at identifying any long-term effects on the mother − child relationship following separation at birth.[31] They state that 'the lack of a connection in this study between disturbed mother − child relationship and duration of stay in special care baby units raises the possibility that factors other than low-birthweight and neonatal separation contribute to disturbed mother − child relationships'. Yet another team set out to check the claim that mothers prone to baby battering are mothers who have not been bonded to their babies soon after delivery.[32] They investigated 80 cases of child abuse with particular reference to the separation of the abusing parents from their newborn infants. Although early separation of parent and infant was found to be common in families under investigation, combinations of other stresses and conflicts were also much in evidence. It is the latter that were thought to have predisposed mothers towards baby battering. The authors do not argue that lack of contact with newborn infants has definitely nothing to do with subsequent battering, but they strongly advocate that for practical purposes 'other stress factors which impair parent – child relationships must also be given attention as important antecedents of non-accidental injury – for example, unstable domestic arrangements, and psychiatric disturbance and immaturity in the parents'. The significance of post-partum separation would be easier to evaluate if we possessed evidence from epidemiological surveys of large populations which indicated the proportion of post-partum separations in which no cases of child abuse had occurred.

The same appeal to evidence is required in relating 'distortions' or 'failures' of bonding to incidents of child abuse. Bonding difficulties are postulated as the intervening variable to explain the link between early separations and neglect or active cruelty to the infant. Assuming that one can identify a failure of bonding, i.e. a failure of mother – child attachment, with the appropriate degree of reliability and validity, how much would it contribute to making a diagnosis? The value of a diagnostic term lies in its descriptive functions, and its implications of aetiology, treatment and prognosis. A label without implications would be somewhat pointless.

Even if we acknowledge an association between failures of bonding and child abuse (and this suggests that we have overcome the formidable difficulty of defining what we mean by bonding – the descriptive implications referred to earlier) there is a trap in believing that such failures are 'necessary' and 'sufficient' causes of child abuse. The problem of (say) the field social worker is that the pseudo-explanatory properties of the term 'bonding' may be a hindrance when he/she is assessing a child in the context of a family with complex social and emotional problems in all of its members. Encountering what he/she perceives to be a failure of bonding, the social worker could be deterred from assessing precisely – in behavioural terms – where and when, and in what situations the problems occur, and indeed, show a bias towards taking the child into care because of what is perceived as an unrelievedly bleak outlook.[33]

The opposite may also occur: an apparently successful bonding, as indicated by affection and nurturant care, may be used as a misleadingly 'favourable' prognostic index. In the case of a 19-month-old child, Jason, who died from injuries after being left alone for hours in a freezing bedroom, the social worker was inclined to believe the mother and her lover (both jailed for five years) when they insisted that they were not harming the child. The social worker pointed out that the mother had great affection for her son and must have been a good mother.[34]

We can never overestimate the difficulties faced by social workers, health visitors, doctors and the police, in making the agonizing decisions that society burdens them with; they have to balance the needs and safety of children and the needs and rights of parents. Theirs is only too often a situation in which they always lose: they are scapegoats when things go tragically (and fortunately, rarely) amiss, and they are unacknowledged when they get things right. It is the opinion of the present writers that preventive child-care action and rehabilitation of the mother or father is hindered rather than helped by introducing the bonding concept, to the extent that it is tied to the critical period immediately after birth. Adhering rigidly to the concept of 'bonding failure' may interfere with the precise assessment of the mother's limitations, which — more often than not — have roots in her past,[35] and the assessment of the intrinsic difficulties of temperament in the child[33] and many other potentially significant contemporary controlling factors, not least the father's role.

It has been argued elsewhere in the book that the nature of a mother's affectional bond (something Jolly describes as the 'flow of feeling from parent to child') is not a sufficient explanation of — or guarantee against — acts of aggression towards the child. Loving mothers have been known to lose self-control and commit acts of cruelty towards their offspring; and rejecting mothers are capable of giving meticulous care. There is a good deal of situation-specificity to the wide range of behaviours referred to generally as 'mothering', as there is also with most other kinds of behaviour. In other words, what we do depends to quite a considerable extent on the places, people and situations that surround us at the time we manifest particular actions.

Although bonding is generally valued as a necessary condition in the provision of optimal conditions for mother — child interactions, and its absence is thought to put the child at risk, we cannot claim that it describes a consistent set of attitudes or actions. There are many inconsistencies, even contradictions, in the literature on parent – child attitudes and relationships and parental child-rearing practice. The global assessments of factors such as parental warmth, hostility and rejection, and also others which are believed to be indicative of bonding or its absence, are too abstract and coarse-grained to capture many of the subtle nuances of maternal behaviour. They fail to show the many variations in behavioural interactions between parents and infants which occur in *particular* situations, and which are necessary if we are to understand the precise relationships between causes and effects.

Nor do they reflect the proactive (as opposed to merely reactive) effect of the child himself and *his* personality. Dunn demonstrated that it was not possible to assume that a correlation between measures of maternal responsiveness is independent of the infant's characteristics. She found continuities over time in mother – child attitudes and relationships which she concludes are best described in terms of interactional styles rather than of exclusively maternal behaviour. [36]

The child psychiatrist, Leon Eisenberg observes that apart from the lack of consistent evidence to support the theory that bonding in the early hours or days post-partum is essential for the development of a normal relationship between mother and infant 'the thesis carries with it the implications of irreversibility and lays a heavy burden on mothers. . . '. [37] We commented in Chapter 3 that the clinical literature – until recently – has tended to neglect the paternal role; 'paternal bonding' is not a term which looms large in the index of books which have a lot to say about maternal bonding. If fathers are kept in 'low profile' then the same can be said of the children. In the crucial business of growing up, there is a two-way traffic in the relationship between parents and child. Yet surprisingly the role of the child in contributing to such unhappy events as his own ill-treatment has been somewhat neglected. Can we really speak of a one-way process with awful or stupid things being done to a passive infant?

Many practitioners addressing themselves to the problem of child abuse, place the main emphasis on parental and, in particular, maternal psychopathology and environmental factors. The role the child can unwittingly play in his own tragic predicament is usually overlooked. Certainly, every mother has an enormous influence on her child's behaviour. By encouraging some activities and discouraging others, she helps shape his personality. But in all sorts of subtle ways, her behaviour is also shaped by the child. And research suggests that there are children who, from birth, show characteristics which make them not only difficult to rear, but also difficult to love. [38] Of late there has come an increasing awareness that some abused children or those who fail to thrive display attributes which are positively aversive to adults and which make them unrewarding and even unlovable to their parents.

As Evelyn Thoman puts it: [39]

Even a normal infant can have behaviour patterns that play a disruptive role in the relationship. For example, an infant has been observed who, from birth through the first weeks of life, showed avoidance responses to being picked up and held. The infant's behaviour was a source of frustration and confusion to the unsuspecting parents. It is obviously difficult for the parent to respond appropriately to the needs of such an infant. And, in turn, the resulting interaction affects the infant's developing behaviours.

Thus, disturbed parent – child relationships and child abuse can be the result of many inter-related factors. What is clear is that child abuse must not be simply ascribed to the lack of 'bonding' during a relatively short period after birth. And yet predictions of future child abuse have seriously been attempted on the basis of what occurs between the mother and her infant just at that time.

Very recently, Montgomery has criticized recommendations currently under consideration to devise procedures to enable us to predict child abuse as early as possible. [40] These have as a cornerstone the claim by Helfer and Kempe that the best predictor of child abuse is maternal behaviour during the perinatal period. [41] Predictions of this kind make use of the medical model of child abuse; the implication is that child abuse is a form of disease inherent in the mother, the signs of which may be discerned long before the symptoms are there for all to see. Furthermore, as we have noted earlier, this 'disease' is often ascribed to the absence of post-partum mother-to-infant bonding. Social workers are warned by Montgomery to 'temper with scepticism their enthusiasm' for attempts to predict child abuse on the basis of early behaviour of the mother towards her young infant.

Adoption and bonding

Childless couples commonly adopt young children and treat them as their own. If the bonding doctrine were to be taken seriously, the prospects for adopted babies would surely be poor. Not only is there no 'blood bond' between adoptive parents and the child, but they have missed out on the allegedly vital hours (not to mention months and sometimes years) of physical and emotional exposure to the youngster. Unlike natural mothers immediately after birth, adoptive mothers would not be in a state of readiness for skin-to-skin contact and rapid bonding to their infants. Can adoptive mothers truly love their children and be strongly attached to them? What sort of parents do adoptive parents make?

Long before the bonding doctrine made its appearance, it had been advocated that, if an infant is to be adopted, it should be adopted as soon after birth as possible. This was to be primarily for the sake of the adopted baby's mental health.[42] It permitted continuity of mothering so beneficial for the child; any discontinuity was thought to involve high risk of disturbed personality development in the child. In any case, however, it was thought that the younger the infant at the time of adoption the easier it would be for the adoptive parents to treat the child as their own; and this would increase the chances of a happy parent – child relationship in the years to come. We cannot quarrel with this view, even if there is no evidence that early adoption is of *crucial* importance either for the child or for the adoptive parents.

For well over 20 years it has been known that from the viewpoint of infantile attachment the first few months of life cannot be critical simply because it takes at least three months before the infant shows unquestioned evidence of discriminating between the familiar and the unfamiliar persons in its environment. Infant-to-mother attachment can develop only when the infant begins to know its mother.[43] From the viewpoint of maternal attachment the age of the adopted baby probably matters a lot but is certainly not the sole determinant of success. What matters a great deal is the yearning for a baby by the adoptive parents, the depth of the emotional experience at the time of adoption, the temperament of the baby, the years of exposure to the adopted child and a whole host of other such factors. However, what cannot be doubted is the intensity of attachment of very many adoptive mothers and fathers.

There is clear evidence that adoptive parents can be good and loving parents; early adoptions are on the whole best, but late adoptions, too, can be remarkably successful.

Tizard reported a study of children who had been in care
throughout their early years; they were followed up on leaving
care.[44] One group of children was adopted, another returned to
their own families. It was found that the latter did less well than the
adopted children, both in the initial stages of settling in and in their
subsequent progress. The reason lay primarily in the attitudes of
the two sets of parents: the adoptive group worked harder at being
parents – possibly just because the child was not their own.

Successful adoption makes nonsense of the unrestrained view of
bonding. Paternal love and attachment likewise put a large question mark over the pessimistic implications of the bonding doctrine. For the doctrine would seem to imply that paternal love is of
a different order and quality from maternal love. The fact that a
female gives birth does not necessarily mean that she invariably
cares for the baby. This is so even in some animal species; male
marmosets, to take one example, carry the infant at all times except
when the infant is feeding.

There have been variations among human groups. Anthropologists tell us that children may not be the special responsibility
of their parents at all in some societies; they may be reared by all
the members of a group living together under one roof or in a small
compact housing unit. Contemporary Western society is witnessing
a massive increase in the number of single-parent families in some
of which the father is the care-giver. The practice of placing
children in need with foster parents is an option generally preferred
to institutional care.

Fostering and bonding

A foster home is a child's substitute family. If the bonding view
were correct, it would hardly be possible for foster parents to form
attachments to their charges. It may well be that it is possible to
look after children satisfactorily without ever becoming attached to
them. But as children may need both care *and* affection if they are
to thrive, then it is clearly better for them to be looked after by persons who show affection and whose affection stems from attachment.

In practice, local authorities have to provide foster homes for children of all ages when their parents are temporarily unable to look after them. Some children are fostered for short periods, others for years. Sometimes the foster mother comes to love her foster child, even though she has to part with it eventually. Hence, the widely publicized heart-rending tug-of-war cases where both the foster parent(s) and the natural parent(s) wish to take charge of the child. If, however, the foster child is not emotionally accepted and perhaps loved in its foster home, then it is liable to be disturbed in its development.[44]

It is noteworthy that a massive re-appraisal is in progress at the present time of fostering as one of the alternatives to institutional care. The realization that good foster parents can succeed in their task, even when the foster child is given to them relatively late, will reinforce the trend towards fostering many categories of disturbed children.

References

1   Welburn, V. (1980) *Postnatal Depression* (London: Fontana).
2   Richards, M.P.M. (1978) 'Possible effects of early separation on later development of children – review'. In Brimblecombe, F.S.W. *et al.* (eds) *Separation and Special-Care Baby Units* (London: Heinemann). Prince, J. *et al.* (1978) 'Contact between babies in incubators and their caretakers'. In Brimblecombe, F.S.W. *et al.* (eds) *Separation and Special-Care Baby Units* (London: Heinemann).
3   Brimblecome, F.S.W. *et al.* (1978) 'Suggestions for the future'. In Brimblecombe, F.S.W. *et al.* (eds) *Separation and Special-Care Baby Units* (London: Heinemann).
4   Clarke, A.M. and Clarke, A.D.B. (eds) (1976) *Early Experience: Myth and Evidence* (London: Open Books).
5   Johns, N. (1971) 'Family reactions to the birth of a child with a congenital abnormality'. *Medical Journal of Australia*, 7, 277 – 82.
6   McMichael, J.K. (1971) *Handicap: A Study of Physically Handicapped Children and their Families* (London: Staples).
7   Burton, L. (1975) *The Family Life of Sick Children* (London: Routledge).
8   Hewett, S. (1970) *The Family and the Handicapped Child* (London: Allen Unwin).
9   Sluckin, W. (1972) *Imprinting and Early Learning* (London: Methuen). Bowlby, J. (1969) *Attachment and Loss, Vol. 1, Attachment* (London: Hogarth Press).

10   Chess, S. (1964) Editorial: '*Mal de mère*', *American Journal of Ortho-psychiatry*, **34**, 613 – 14.

11   Kanner, L. (1943) 'Autistic disturbances of affective contact', *Nervous Child*, **2**, 217 – 50.

12   Bettelheim, B. (1967) *The Empty Fortress* (New York: Free Press).

13   Eberhardy, F. (1967) 'The view from "the couch"', *Journal of Child Psychology and Psychiatry*, **8**, 257 – 63.

14   Cox, A. *et al.* (1975) 'A comparative study of infantile autism and specific developmental language disorder. II. Parental characteristics', *British Journal of Psychiatry*, **126**, 146 – 59.

15   Wing, L. (1971) *Autistic Children* (London: Constable).

16   Tinbergen, E.A. and Tinbergen, N. (1972) *Early Childhood Autism: An Ethological Approach* (Berlin: Paul).

17   Smith, S.M. (1975) *The Battered Child Syndrome* (London: Butterworth).

18   Patton, R. and Gardner, L.I. (1962) 'Influence of family environment on growth: the syndrome of maternal deprivation', *Paediatrics*, **30**, 957.

19   Gardner, L.I. (1972) 'Deprivation dwarfism', *Scientific American*, **227** (1), 76 – 82.

20   Pollitt, E., Eichler, A.W. and Chan, C-K. (1975) 'Psychosocial development and behavior of mothers of failure-to-thrive children', *American Journal of Orthopsychiatry*, **45**, 525 – 36.

21   Vietze, P.M. *et al.* (1980) 'Newborn behavioural and interactional characteristics of nonorganic failure-to-thrive infants'. In Field, J.M. (ed.) *High-Risk Infants and Children: Adult and Peer Interactions* (London: Academic Press).

22   Iwaniec, D. and Herbert, M. (1982) 'The assessment and treatment of children who fail to thrive', *Social Work Today*, **13** (22), 8 – 12.

23   Valman, H.B. (1980) 'The first year of life: mother – infant bonding', *British Medical Journal*, **280**, 308 – 10.

24   Klaus, M. and Kennell, J. (1976) *Maternal – Infant Bonding* (St Louis: Mosby).

25   Lynch, M.A. and Roberts, J. (1977) 'Predicting child abuse: signs of bonding failure in the maternity hospital', *British Medical Journal*, **1**, 624 – 36.
      Hunter, R.S., Kilstrom, N., Kraybill, E.N. and Loda, F. (1978) 'Antecedents of child abuse and neglect in premature infants: a prospective study in a newborn intensive care unit', *Paediatrics*, **61**, 629 – 35.

26   Jolly, H. (1978) 'The importance of 'bonding' for newborn baby, mother . . . and father', *Nursing Mirror*, August 31, 19 – 21.

27   Harlow, H. F. and Harlow, M. R. (1965) 'The affectional systems'. In Schrier, A.M. *et al.* (eds) *Behavior of Nonhuman Primates,* Vol. 2 (New York: Academic Press).

28   Elmer, E. and Gregg, G.S. (1967) 'Developmental characteristics of abused children', *Pediatrics*, **40**, 596 – 602.
      Klein, M. and Stern, L. (1971) 'Low birth weight and the battered child syndrome', *American Journal of Diseases of Children*, **122**, 15.

Lynch, M.A. *et al.* (1976) 'Child abuse: early warning in the maternity hospital', *Developmental Medicine and Child Neurology*, **18**, 759 – 66.

29 Argles, P. (1980) 'Attachment and child abuse', *British Journal of Social Work*, **10**, 33 – 42.

30 Gaines, R., Sangrund, A., Green, A.H. and Power, E. (1978) 'Etiological factors in child maltreatment: a multivariate study of abusing, neglecting and normal mothers', *Journal of Abnormal Psychology*, **87**, 531 – 40.

31 Collingwood, J. and Alberman, E. (1979) 'Separation at birth and the mother – child relationship', *Developmental Medicine and Child Neurology*, **21**, 608 – 17.

32 Cater, J.I. and Easton, P.M. (1980) 'Separation and other stress in child abuse', *Lancet*, **2**, 972 – 4.

33 Herbert, M. (1981) *The Behavioural Treatment of Problem Children: A Practice Manual* (London: Academic Press).

34 Fogarty, M. (1981) 'Jason: Why the police were not called in', *Social Work Today*, **13**, 2.

35 Lynch, M.A., Roberts, J. and Gordon, M., (1976) 'Child abuse: early warning in the maternity hospital, *Developmental Medicine and Child Neurology*, **18**, 759 – 66.

36 Dunn, J.B. (1975) 'Consistency and change in styles of mothering'. In *Parent – Infant Interaction, CIBA Foundation Symposium*, **33**, (Amsterdam: Elsevier-Excerpta Medica).

37 Eisenberg, L. (1981) 'Social context of child development', *Paediatrics*, **68**, 705 – 11.

38 Herbert, M. (1978) *Conduct Disorders of Childhood and Adolescence: A Behavioural Approach to Assessment and Treatment* (Chichester: Wiley.)

39 Thoman, E.B. (1975) 'How a rejecting baby affects mother – infant synchrony'. In *Parent – Infant Interaction, CIBA Foundation* Symposium, **33** (Amsterdam: Elsevier – Excerpta Medica).

40 Montgomery, S. (1982) 'Problems in the perinatal prediction of child abuse', *British Journal of Social Work*, **12**, 189 – 96.

41 Helfer, R.E. and Kempe, C.H. (1976) *Child Abuse and Neglect* (Cambridge, Mass.: Ballinger).

42 Bowlby, J. (1958) 'The nature of the child's tie to his mother', *International Journal of Psychoanalysis*, **39**, 550 – 73.
    Bowlby, J.D. (1969) *Attachment and Loss, Vol. 1, Attachment,* (London: Hogarth Press).

43 Schaffer, H.R. (1977) *Mothering* (London: Open Books/Fontana).

44 Tizard, B. (1977) *Adoption: A Second Chance* (London: Open Books).

6

The development of parental attachments

If there are no grounds for believing that mother-to-infant bonding occurs rapidly through mother – infant contact during a short-duration critical period after birth, then how does bonding develop? This is a pertinent question because there can be no doubting that, generally speaking, mothers are in a powerful manner emotionally attached to their offspring. And not only mothers; fathers, too, form strong bonds with their children. Grandparents commonly appear to be attached to some extent to their grandchildren; and aunts and uncles can show signs of attachment to their nieces and nephews. Adults are known sometimes to be attached to children that are not their blood-relations, and this is especially so in the case of adoptive parents and foster parents. Thus, attachment is a matter of degree, not an all-or-none phenomenon; we shall examine this issue more closely later in this chapter. It is well known that specific attachments may be observed in the animal world as well as in the human species. Can the study of species evolution shed light on the nature of maternal and similar attachments.

Before attempting to answer this question we must draw attention to a distinction which is important, if rather obvious. One tends to talk somewhat loosely about maternal bonding, maternal attachment, maternal behaviour, maternal instinct and so forth. The simple fact is that protective, care-giving behaviour by adult individuals, female and male, directed towards the young and helpless can readily be observed in mammalian species, including our own. In everyday speech this would commonly be called mothering, or maternal behaviour; other phrases, such as maternal instinct, or parental behaviour, are also used. As will be seen later, the term, instinct, presents some problems. For the present, therefore, let us adopt the phrase, *maternal behaviour*, to refer to the way that adults, animal or human, often act towards infants in general. But let there be no doubt that in the case of human beings we are just as interested, if not more so, in maternal feelings as in maternal behaviour.

Clearly, people can experience warm, protective feelings towards infants, without displaying them. These feelings, overt or covert, are, however, not as a rule as intense as the love one has for one's own child or children. This love of the child one is attached to has a quality of its own. We just do not feel the same way about a young stranger as we do about a friend, a member of one's family, and especially one's own child. This special feeling, and the behaviour associated with it, we may call *maternal attachment*. Other descriptive phrases of roughly equivalent meaning have also been used, e.g. maternal bond, parental attachment, and so on.

Maternal attachment is maternal behaviour plus something additional. Broadly speaking, maternal behaviour is general and indiscriminate. Maternal attachment starts as maternal behaviour; but with time, it becomes established as something highly specific; it is an emotional attachment to another particular being.

The evolution of behaviour

Students of animal behaviour, ethologists and, more recently, those who call themselves sociobiologists, have laid emphasis on viewing social behaviour in its evolutionary perspective. This brings out more clearly the adaptive significance of the many different types of social behaviour. Parental, care-giving behaviour contributes greatly to the survival of the young. However, such behaviour endangers the adults indulging in it. By caring for the young — sheltering them, feeding them, defending them and so forth — the adult runs the risk of itself perishing, and thus leaving no progeny. On the other hand, if the parents, whose genes are carriers of the make-up in which parental behaviour is rooted, do survive, then their offspring, too, will show parental behaviour; and this will contribute to the survival of the species.

The balance between individual survival and species survival is a very fine one; it can easily be tipped one way or the other. It is of some relevance that maternal behaviour may be regarded as a form of altruistic behaviour; and the question as to how innate altruism in the broadest sense, both in animals and in man, could be brought about through natural selection is somewhat puzzling and is much debated, particularly by sociobiologists.[1]

We have implied that in considering maternal behaviour we are dealing with something innate. We may note straight away that this is a gross oversimplification, although partially true; we shall turn to this particular question in the next section of the present chapter. For the present, we can note that more of the offspring of the caring parents will live than of the less caring ones; and furthermore, individuals lacking in the disposition to bond to their young will not have as good a chance of passing on their genes to succeeding generations. The tendency to form attachments must be rooted in the physical make-up of the individual, inhering perhaps mainly in her/his nervous system. Thus we must expect the proneness to parent-to-infant bonding to be *in some measure* built into all of us.

Is there a maternal instinct?

We have just indicated that maternal behaviour and the tendency to form maternal attachments are in part genetically determined. This brings us immediately into the heart of the old debate of nature *versus* nurture, or instinct *versus* learning. The debate has at times loomed very large in psychology and related disciplines; but for the most part it has tended to be unproductive. This has been so mainly because it posed the problem in an either – or fashion; in other words, the question which was asked called for an answer which could not sensibly be given. For it is impossible to conceive of an organism wholly unaffected by its environment or, again, totally uninfluenced by its inheritance. Any creature's structure as well as behaviour will be of necessity partly influenced by its genes and partly by its experience of the environment. The relative contributions of the genetic and environmental influences, although not readily susceptible to quantification, clearly vary enormously; but both kinds of contribution there must be.

As we move up the evolutionary scale, the innately determined modes of behaviour are less and less dominant, and the individually acquired or learned modes of behaviour are more and more in evidence. The contribution of nurture to behaviour, including social behaviour, is undoubtedly greatest in the human species; but this does not mean that our inherited nature has no part, or only very little part, to play.

Maternal behaviour is well developed in many species. In mammals, including monkeys and apes, our nearest animal relatives, the normal tendency (pathology is considered in the last section of this chapter) to care for the young manifests itself in various forms in individuals that have had no prior opportunity to learn the skills of mothering; maternal behaviour must therefore be regarded as at least to some extent inherited, innate or instinctive. However, in the human species such behaviour is at the same time highly modifiable and subject to environmental influences, involving much learning. Now tied up with the discipline of comparative psychology is the field of study known as behaviour genetics, or psychogenetics. In relation to animal behaviour this is concerned with selective breeding for behaviour characteristics such as timidity, docility, care-giving behaviour and the like. With regard to the study of human psychological characteristics or personality traits, we cannot of course turn for help to experimental psychogenetics. This does not mean, however, that we are unable to learn anything about the genetic roots of some features of human social behaviour, including maternal behaviour and the tendency to form maternal attachments.

Maternal, care-giving behaviour has been extensively studied in mammals for a long time.[2] It could be described as instinctive in that it makes its appearance when the individual reaches a certain stage in its development, and it does not require any learning. However, the adjective instinctive − let alone the noun, instinct − is somewhat disreputable in scientific circles. It must be said that it is disreputable for quite a good reason. The word, instinctive, when used at one time, was confusing because it meant at least two different things, if not more. In some cases instinctive behaviour meant emerging patterns of behaviour which did not depend on any prior experience. But in other cases, instinctive behaviour meant a variety of motivational forces underlying the behaviour in question (e.g. self-assertion, acquisitiveness, curiosity).

These different usages were responsible for a good deal of conceptual muddle in the literature. Worse still, to say that a certain kind of behaviour was instinctive often sounded dogmatic and explained very little, if anything. And yet, it may well be argued that there is no necessity to avoid altogether using in scientific discourse common words like instinct. Such terms − and instinct is only one of them − are clearly ambiguous and misleading to some degree;

but they can also be useful. In the present context there is much to be said for referring to maternal behaviour in a simple manner as instinctive, or at any rate as having an instinctive component, provided that it is agreed that we mean by this that such behaviour is in some considerable measure genetically determined. A monkey has to *learn* circus tricks and the process of acquiring such skills may be a lengthy one; but a female monkey that has given birth to an infant does not need to learn mothering – it knows what to do instinctively, although its mothering skills can and do to some degree improve through experience.

Human beings would not perhaps be very good at mothering without some, or much, learning. We do not really know how capable an entirely untutored mother would be to take care of her infant; but we may guess that she would not be completely helpless. In so far as she would have some ability to look after her infant, her mothering could be called instinctive. Moreover, the human mother's behaviour towards her infant might also be described as instinctive because of her motivational-emotional state at the time. Her motives and feelings cannot be specified in any exact manner, and her own reports could be rather unreliable; nevertheless it is difficult to believe that her propensity to provide care-giving is wholly unconnected with her genetic endowment.

As we have said earlier, there are scientific objections to the use of the word, instinct, especially in the context of human behaviour. Perhaps a less controversial term than maternal instinct is required to highlight the role of the genetic contribution to maternal behaviour. However, it is one thing to object to the term, maternal instinct, and another thing altogether to argue that there is just no such thing as maternal instinct. The latter is a position which has some popular appeal; it holds that maternal behaviour is purely culturally determined.[3] Now at least some of those who adopt this anti-maternal-instinct stance probably do not quite mean that nature plays no part whatsoever in maternal behaviour. Rather their message is concerned with day-to-day practice. And the essence of the message is that both the father and the mother should share equally in the 'mothering' of their children, or, as it is nowadays sometimes put, in the process of 'parenting'. If that is the central feature of the anti-maternal-instinct position which writers such as Badinter[3] adopt, then this would be difficult to argue against; although some writers hold that the mother's role in relation to young children is a key one.[4] Of course, a total denial of a genetically controlled element in human care-giving behaviour — call it maternal or parental — is a position which is untenable.

Affectional bonds between individuals

Over a decade ago an eminent American psychologist, Harry Harlow, wrote a book about 'learning to love'. Love defies precise definition; but to Harlow it means 'affectional feelings for others'. His book begins with a description of several different 'affectional systems'.[5] The first he lists is 'maternal love, the love of the mother for her child' — the very centre of our own interest. It is instructive to note the other affectional systems; one of them is paternal love, 'the love of the adult male for his family'; others are 'the love of child for child' (and adolescent for adolescent), and, of course, heterosexual love. As a student of both animal and human behaviour, Harlow discusses the different affectional systems in a comparative manner; and the focus is on 'learning to love', that is the *development* of attachments. In this section and the two subsequent ones of the present chapter, the centre of our interest will be the growth of maternal and similar attachments; in the context of our discussion, growth refers more to learning than to maturing.

Whether human females are more responsive than human males to infants in general is a moot point. They display parental behaviour more readily, but this might be only a cultural influence, although conclusive evidence is hard to come by. It is apparent, however, that some human mothers have hardly any maternal feelings towards their newborns. Even so, they gradually develop these feelings in relation to their own babies when interaction — cooing, smiling and so on — begins to be established between them and their infants. Some mothers report falling in love at first sight with their newborn infants. It is impossible to question the existence of this type of experience. It must be borne in mind, however, that sometimes our experiences conform to our own expectations or the expectations of others. In any case, a new baby is liable to evoke in most of us a natural nurturance which manifests itself in both tender feelings and care-giving action. A love at first sight can grow stronger still with time. That is what we may think, but objective measures of love intensity are not readily available.

The concept of love, at first sight or otherwise, in contemporary

Western culture, has some interesting features. Heterosexual love, for example, tends to be conceived of as the outcome of a spontaneous emotional reaction between two people of suddenly being gripped by an irresistible feeling. By contrast, in some other cultures, where marriage partners are chosen for each other, love is said to be exclusively the result of an act of will and commitment.[6] Thus, it is assumed that one can learn to love others provided the circumstances are right. This idea is not entirely absent even in our culture. Dr Spock, for instance, stresses that it takes time for parents to fall in love with their new baby, that 'love for the baby comes gradually'.[7]

The growth of love is partly a function of the mother's sheer *exposure* to her baby; it is also facilitated by the baby's developing repertoire of responses to stimulation: tactile, visual, auditory, etc. As Harlow puts it, 'mother love is indiscriminate, and in human mothers often absent, at the outset'. Specific love tends to develop slowly but surely. The bond to the child gradually grows stronger and stronger. Very, very much later it may weaken, but it probably never vanishes. We may say in passing that the course of the growth of paternal love appears to be essentially similar; but we shall have a little more to say about this later in the chapter.

Exposure learning and conditioning

We have already mentioned that the mother's mere exposure to her baby makes a contribution towards the development of a bond to the baby. We may go further and say that exposure, although not the only factor in attachment, is probably the central one. This is a view that emerges from studies of exposure learning. Somewhat surprisingly perhaps, the evidence is that liking for anybody and anything is initially a direct function of familiarity.[8] The adage that 'familiarity breeds contempt' does not run counter to all evidence; beyond a certain point continuing exposure does make for a decline in liking in certain types of situation, but that is another matter.[9] The central feature of exposure learning is that the individual, animal or human, forms an attachment to a given figure not because she/he is rewarded for it, but because the attachment is, as it were, self-rewarding. This is not to say that external reinforcement of attachment is ineffective. External rewards strengthen attachments but are not a *sine qua non*; mere exposure is enough. A foster mother, for example, may be paid for her services and may be praised if her charges thrive; this may help her to develop positive feelings towards her foster children; but an adoptive mother's care for her children might get no such clear reinforcements, and yet she may come to love her children dearly.

The same view of bonding emerges even more strongly from the important and influential attachment theory of John Bowlby[10]. This theory was originally put forward to account for infantile attachments to adults. More generally it is 'a way of conceptualizing the propensity of human beings to make strong affectional bonds to particular others and of explaining the many forms of emotional distress and personality disturbance, including anxiety, anger, depression and emotional detachment, to which unwilling separation and loss give rise'. With regard to learning Bowlby has the following to say:

Whereas learning to distinguish the familiar from the strange is a key process in the development of attachment, the conventional rewards and punishments used by experimental psychologists play only a small part. Indeed, an attachment can develop despite repeated punishment from the attachment figure.

The last sentence, well borne out by observational and experimental evidence, is a telling one. Although Bowlby had in mind infantile attachment, maternal attachment, too, can have severely punishing consequences: hard work, frustration and seeming ingratitude. Despite such consequences, maternal attachment has proved resilient, persistent and enduring.

This having been said, the role of conditioning in developing and cementing maternal attachment must now be emphasized. In terms of classical conditioning, the appearance of young infants, and the sounds they make, are unconditioned stimuli which evoke maternal feelings and mothering behaviour. The ethologists have drawn attention to certain infantile visual characteristics which release caregiving responses, such as large head in proportion to the body, large forehead relative to the face, large eyes, short and thick limbs, rounded body shape, etc.[11] Some behavioural attributes, e.g. clumsiness, have been said to help in releasing mothering. Incidentally, young animals, too, have many of these features, and therefore evoke unconditionally care-giving behaviour in people.

Now classical conditioning occurs when an initially neutral stimulus is repeatedly associated with, or signals, an unconditioned stimulus. Under such circumstances a neutral stimulus becomes the conditioned stimulus, and is thereby capable of eliciting behaviour which was originally displayed only in response to the unconditioned stimulus. In the type of situation we are considering, caregiving behaviour is a response to the releasers inherent in all infants, as mentioned in the previous paragraph. What of the conditioned stimuli?

We may theorize that the specific, neutral, non-releasing characteristics of one's own baby — for instance, its voice, its clothes, etc. — come to be the conditioned stimuli which by themselves can eventually evoke maternal feelings and behaviour. In this manner, one's child, and literally everything associated with it, stimulate maternal affection. For this reason one's own child gradually becomes more powerful in evoking its mother's love than are other children; other children present only unconditioned stimuli, whereas one's own child presents both unconditioned *and* conditioned stimuli. Such conditioning is a gradual process and may go on hand-in-hand with the gradual exposure learning which is at the back of the steady growth of maternal attachment. A story has been told of two newborn infants having been in error exchanged in hospital between two mothers. When some weeks later the error was discovered, the mothers did not want their own babies back; they were already so very strongly attached to their charges.

Classical, Pavlovian conditioning is only one of the learning processes which may be implicated in the strengthening of the mother-to-infant bond. Another type of conditioning, known as instrumental or operant (we need not concern ourselves here with the rather subtle differences between the two) may also be at work. This form of conditioning typically occurs when some of one's actions are followed by a reward while others are not. The rewarded actions are thus reinforced and become more frequent and established.

In the context of the mother — infant relationship, everything that the mother does for the child which benefits it is *ipso facto* reinforcing for the mother. As the mother gets to know her child, she finds out how best to care for it — feed it, keep it warm, keep it clean, etc. — and the more effective her mothering activities the more they become stamped in. Feelings of satisfaction become more and more closely associated with her child and this helps to strengthen her relationship with the child, her attachment to it. Again, such a process would be a gradual one. Incidentally, failure-to-thrive children are relatively less rewarding to look after. For this reason their mothers sometimes show less maternal attachment. It has been suggested that such children do not thrive because they are rejected by their mothers. As we saw in the last chapter, the opposite may be nearer the truth; the seeming rejection, or relative lack of attachment, is the result rather than the cause of the failure-to-thrive condition.

In addition to conditioning, cultural influences may be important in encouraging maternal attachments. Much learning is not, as it were, direct as in exposure learning, classical conditioning and operant conditioning, but indirect or vicarious, as in social, observational learning and imitation. Young mothers watch other more experienced ones; they remember perhaps how their own mothers acted. They observe and imitate, and thus many characteristically cultural features of mothering are perpetuated. In so far as strong mother-to-infant bonds are a feature of our culture, this feature is likely to be maintained through observational learning.

Clearly, there could be many factors in the mother – infant situation which help develop maternal attachment. We cannot be sure what is the relative contribution of each, and we may be quite unaware of the operation of some contributory factors. What is extremely unlikely, however, is that mother-to-infant bonding occurs very rapidly, or that it occurs mainly through skin-to-skin contact, rather than gradually as a result of well known forms of learning, including exposure, imitation and conditioning.

Harlow suggests that mother-love develops over a period of several months.[5] On the other hand, the allegedly ethological, sensitive-period theory of bonding suggests that mother-love is established very rapidly. [If this be so, then 'nature' has arranged matters in a most risky fashion. What survival value is there in fashioning something as vital as a mother's attachment to her child within a relatively short space of time during which a woman is particularly vulnerable — perhaps exhausted, weak, even ill or depressed? Such an all-or-nothing arrangement would make for a surprisingly fragile link in the chain of events which see the dependent human infant through to mature self-sufficiency.]

* revealing sentence

It would make sense in adaptational terms if problems of early adjustment did not have long-term sequelae. Dunn carried out a longitudinal study of 70 mother – baby pairs – observations being recorded at various intervals over a 30-week time-span.[12] Apart from demonstrating the extreme difficulty of basing predictions of future relationships on the early mother – infant interaction, Dunn concludes that the absence of a correlation between coordination measures from the early feeds and the later consistent maternal measures 'suggests that the post-partum period, rather than being a sensitive period, may be a time when the relationship between the mother and baby is buffered against difficulties of adjustment'.

There would seem to be another benefit if maternal attachment proceeded on a gradual rather than rapid basis. In the case of the infant's death in the perinatal period, the mother is not so bonded that she cannot continue to realize her other care-giving tasks and, indeed, her reproductive potential. Dunn's findings suggest that it may take three or four weeks for mother and infant to settle to a characteristic pattern. Given the importance attached by some practitioners to finding ways of assessing mother – child relationships for potential difficulties such as child abuse, it may be more valid to look for indices of adjustment at this later stage.

Richards states that 'the idea of separation does not in itself constitute a psychological theory – it merely describes a particular state of affairs'.[13] What we do know about the interactions of mothers and their babies in the early post-partum days is that there is an immense range of individual differences in their coordination and smoothness. We still lack evidence about the long-term implications of these early differences for mother-and-baby pairs who remain together from birth onwards, as well as for pairs separated for varying periods of time. Without hard evidence about the former group, it is not possible to be sure whether qualitative differences in the early adjustment and interaction may have significant consequences for the evolving relationship, even when mother and infant are not separated. Although the cry for more research is a valid one, the difficulties of testing the hypothesis that early separation has long-term consequences are awesome. As mothers, these days, are not usually separated from their neonates without justifiable reasons, it is almost impossible to make up separation and non-separation groups that are comparable in all other respects.

If we are to understand more fully how maternal attachment

develops, we must bear in mind that it develops in the context of continual mother – infant *interactions*. This has been mentioned earlier in the book, and emphasised by many other authors, but by no-one more than by Robert Hinde.[14] Whatever the mother does in relation to her baby, affects the baby; and the baby's behaviour thus affected, in turn, influences the mother's next action, and so on. Even in the case of very young infants, these interactions are of considerable complexity. This makes each sequence of interactions for a given mother – infant pair quite unique. Thus, the course of development of maternal attachment in each individual case is unique, even though the same general 'laws' of learning are operative in all cases.

What is also essential for our understanding of the development of maternal attachment is what mothers report about their feelings as the love for their babies grows, or fails to grow. One small-scale survey revealed that, of the 97 mothers who had delivered their babies two months previously, 40 said that they felt love for their infants during pregnancy, 23 at birth, 26 during the first week of the baby's life, and 8 after the end of the first week.[15] The mothers also reported that their love grew stronger with time: 30 thought this was at birth, 29 – during the first two weeks, and 10 – during the second two weeks; a further 28 believed that their love did not grow greater. As the author says, 'There is great variation here, and it suggests that for many women the development of maternal love is a fairly gradual affair.' The limitations of such surveys are obvious enough: the reports of mothers reflect their impressions, which can, of course, be influenced by their expectations; and their expectations are generally influenced by what they have been led to believe about the onset of love. Nevertheless, information of this type could contribute some vital pieces to the solution of the jigsaw puzzle that maternal attachment is in each individual case.

The role of the father

We have repeatedly talked about maternal attachment as well as parental attachment, implying that adult-to-infant bonding is not unique to the mother. We have indicated that attachment is a matter of degree and that its strength depends on many factors, one of them being the degree of exposure of the adult to the infant, or familiarity of the adult with the infant. We may now be more explicit and suggest that father-to-infant attachment is not so different in kind from maternal attachment. Certainly paternal behaviour soon after the birth of a baby very often resembles in many details maternal behaviour.[16] Paternal attachment, however, often (but not invariably) appears to be less strong than maternal attachment. There are some good reasons for this.

In the first place, general responsiveness of the human male to infants tends to be less marked. It would not altogether surprise us if there were genetic factors responsible for this. In many, but not all, species of primates males are less nurturing to the young than females, although males tend to be protective both towards the females and their young. Undoubtedly, however, the role of the human male in relation to the young is enormously influenced by culture, custom and convention. Until relatively recent times in Western and Central Europe men were not expected to perform certain domestic duties, including the feeding of young infants, changing nappies, etc. The situation in this regard is at present changing rapidly. It may be that without the cultural overlay men's feelings and responses towards babies would not be all that different from women's. If, for whatever reason, the responsiveness of males to babies is on the whole less strong than that of females, then specific paternal attachments would be initially somewhat handicapped in their development. In the end they would not perhaps reach the intensity of maternal attachments.

Secondly in the usual Western family the extent of contact between father and baby is less than that between mother and baby. This may be regrettable, but it is a fact that cannot be overlooked. In the circumstances, paternal attachments have less opportunity to grow at the same rate as maternal attachments; exposure learning, classical conditioning, operant learning, imitation and the rest have less time to operate. No wonder that paternal attachments often seem less emotional than maternal attachments and dominate men's lives less than they do women's lives. What perhaps is surprising is that, despite everything, the attachments of fathers to their offspring are, for the most part, so extremely strong. To say, however, that paternal attachment is essentially of the same kind as maternal attachment does not imply that the father's role in our society is basically no different from that of the mother's. The interested reader may pursue further the topic of the father's role by referring to a recent extensive volume, edited by M. E. Lamb. [17]

The psychopathology of maternal attitudes

Our understanding of the nature of maternal affection and rejection is sadly limited. This lack of knowledge is particularly regrettable when we are faced with the enigma of the mother who repudiates her infant. It may be an unacceptable notion, given the widespread myths about 'mother-love' and its sanctity and universality, that there are women who feel little or nothing for their offspring. Indeed, a very small number (relatively speaking) express outright revulsion and hostility for their children.

We know that many factors in the mother's background can influence how she will relate to her child;[18] but that is a far cry from being able to predict a particular woman's feelings for her baby from known circumstances, especially those extreme cases of pathological indifference or loathing. The factors which make for a rejecting mother are likely to be multiple and additive in their influence. They may be, in part, situational. A baby might be born at a particularly bad time for the mother − a time of emotional vulnerability and/or financial hardship. The infant may lead to disharmony between the mother and a pathologically jealous husband, to the extent of threatening the marriage. Mothers have become rejecting when their babies are unresponsive, and indeed, in some of their attributes, quite unlovable.[19] Doubtless there are temperamental, for example narcissistic, aspects in the make-up of some mothers which make it difficult for them to love anyone but themselves; there is little room left over for babies. But rejection is not a fixed characteristic. Feelings can and do change.

Studies of parent − child relationships have been made possible by using special psychological measures and statistical techniques of analysis to reduce the rich variety of maternal behaviour to a few main dimensions.[20]

There are two main underlying, independent dimensions of parental attitudes and behaviours:

a) attitudes which are 'warm' (or loving) at one extreme, and 'rejecting' (or hostile) at the other;

b) attitudes which are restrictive (controlling) at one extreme, and permissive (encouraging autonomy) at the other.

The combination of *loving and controlling* attitudes is indexed by behaviours which are restrictive, overprotective, possessive or over-indulgent in content; *loving and permissive* attitudes are shown by actions which are accepting, cooperative and democratic. The combination of *rejecting and controlling* attitudes is indexed by behaviours which are authoritarian, dictatorial, demanding or antagonistic; *rejecting and permissive* attitudes are indicated by actions which are detached, indifferent, neglectful or hostile.

The outcomes of these combinations − trends of course − are various but most worrying in the case of the last-mentioned category.[21]

For some children rejection means callous and indifferent neglect or positive hostility and cruelty from the parents. This rejection does not always take the form of physical cruelty or negligence. It may be emotional and subtle, so that the child comes to believe that his very existence makes his parents unhappy, and that he is an unmitigated nuisance and something to be devalued.

A rejecting parent tends not only to discourage his child's demands for nurturance, but also to punish his dependent behaviours. One would expect, therefore, that more severe forms of rejection would lead children to suppress such behaviour. This is reflected in the finding that aggressive boys who have undergone a good deal of parental rejection show much less dependent behaviour than non-aggressive boys who have been accepted by their parents.[21] There is an exception. If the parents withhold, or are meagre with their attentions and care, but do not actually punish dependent behaviour, they are likely to *intensify* the child's needs for attention and care. The more a child is 'pushed away' (figuratively speaking) the more he clings for dear life.

Several investigations have looked at the effects of a woman's childhood experiences on her own subsequent maternal attitudes; they suggest a relationship between disrupted childhood and family life (separation, rejection, parental disharmony) and difficulties of adapting to a maternal role.[22] Kempe and Kempe[23] report that the most consistent features of the histories of abusive families is the repetition, from one generation to the next, of a pattern of abuse, neglect and parent loss or deprivation. They admit that 'no one knows quite how the ability to be a parent is passed on from one generation to the next. Probably the most significant channel is the experience of having been sympathetically parented, of having experienced what it feels like to be an infant, helpless but cherished and nurtured into childhood.'

An understanding of 'affectionless' mothers requires a more general understanding of so-called affectionless personalities in people who are sometimes said to suffer from psychopathic disorders. It is quite likely that adults who are capable only of relating to other adults (e.g. spouses) in a superficial, exploitive and hostile manner, show similar relationships with their children.[24]

As is usual in these matters, there is an opposite extreme. Not only can there be too little maternal care, there can also be excessive mother – child attachment and contact. In such a case, the child may sleep in the same room as his mother for years. She tends to fondle him excessively, watch over him constantly, and prevent him taking risks or acting in an independent manner. She fusses a lot about his health by over-medicating and over-dressing him. His mind is made up for him more often than not. In return for absolute obedience, she may over-indulge his every whim, in an attempt to prolong his childhood and keep him tied to her apron strings. Overprotective mothers frequently alternate between dominating and submitting to their children.[25] Such overprotection is frequently cited among the causes of emotional problems, and is sometimes referred to colloquially as 'smother love' or 'momism'.

The proposed precursors of excessive maternal attachment are several, and they are also speculative. It may be that a child is infantilized and 'held onto' because he perhaps is particularly 'precious'; he follows a prolonged period of infertility, a series of miscarriages, or the loss of a sibling. Some mothers are anxious by temperament; others by circumstances as when an infant is ill or disabled – or simply because he is the first-born, arriving when the parents are apprehensive 'learners'.[26]

References

1 Hinde, R.A. (1974) *Biological Bases of Human Social Behaviour* (New York: McGraw-Hill).
   Barash, D.P. (1977) *Sociobiology and Behaviour* (New York: Elsevier).

2 Rheingold, H.L. (ed.) (1963) *Maternal Behavior in Mammals* (New York: Wiley).
   Gubernick, D.J. and Klopfer, P.H. (eds) (1981) *Parental Care in Mammals* (New York: Plenum)

3 Badinter, E. (1981) *The Myth of Motherhood* (London: Souvenir Press).

4 Kellmer Pringle, M.L. (2nd ed. 1971) *Deprivation and Education* (London: Longman).

5 Harlow, H.F. (1971) *Learning to Love* (San Francisco: Albion).

6 Fromm, E. (1957) *The Art of Loving* (London: Allen and Unwin).

7 Spock, B. (1957) *Baby and Child Care* (New York: Pocket Books).

8 Sluckin, W. (1972) *Imprinting and Early Learning.* (London: Methuen).

9 Sluckin, W., Hargreaves, D.J. and Colman, A.M. (1982) 'Some experimental studies of familiarity and liking', *Bulletin of the British Psychological Society*, **35**, 189 – 94.

10 Bowlby, J. (1969) *Attachment and Loss, Vol. 1 Attachment* (London: Hogarth Press).
Bowlby, J. (1977) 'The making and breaking of affectional bonds: I. Aetiology and psychopathology in the light of attachment theory', *British Journal of Psychiatry*, **130**, 201 – 10.

11 Eibl-Eibesfeldt, I. (1970) *Ethology: The Biology of Behavior* (New York: Holt, Rinehart and Winston).

12 Dunn, J.B. (1975) 'Consistency and change in styles of mothering'. In *Parent – Infant Interaction, CIBA Foundation Symposium*, Vol. 33, (Amsterdam: Elsevier-Excerpta Medica).

13 Richards, M.P.M. (1975) 'Early separation'. In Lewin R. (ed.) *Child Alive* (London: Temple Smith).

14 Hinde, R.A. (1979) *Towards Understanding Relationships* (London: Academic Press).

15 MacFarlane, A. (1977) *The Psychology of Childbirth* (London: Fontana/Open Books).

16 Sullivan, J. and McDonald, D. (1979) 'Newborn orientated paternal behaviour'. In Howells, J.G. (ed.) *Modern Perspectives in the Psychiatry of Infancy* (New York: Brunner/Mazel).

17 Lamb, M.E. (ed.) (1981) *The Role of the Father in Child Development* (New York: Wiley).

18 Robson, K.S. (1981) 'A study of mothers' emotional reactions to their newborn babies'. Unpublished Ph.D. dissertation, University of London.

19 Herbert, M. and Iwaniec, D. (1977) 'Children who are hard to love', *New Society*, **4**, April 21.

20 Schaefer, E.S. (1959) 'A circumplex model for maternal behaviour', *Journal of Abnormal and Social Psychology*, **59**, 226 – 35.

21 Becker, W.C. (1964) 'Consequences of different kinds of parental discipline'. In Hoffman, M.L. and Hoffman, L.W. (eds) *Review of Child Development Research* (New York: Russell Sage Foundation).

22 Rutter, M. and Madge, N. (1976) *Cycles of Disadvantage* (London: Heinemann).

23 Kempe, R.S. and Kempe, C.H. (1978) *Child Abuse* (London: Fontana/Open Books).

24 Craft, M.J. (ed.) (1966) *Psychopathic Disorders and their Assessment* (Oxford: Pergamon).
25 Levy, D.M. (1943) *Maternal Overprotection* (New York: Columbia University Press).
26 Herbert, M. (1975) *Problems of Childhood: A Complete Guide for All Concerned*. (London: Pan) (see Chapter 24).

7

Some lessons to be learned: the good news

We have covered up to this point quite a lot of ground. We mentioned the changing ideas as to how best to deal with situations surrounding birth. We discussed the ramifications of the maternal bonding concept. We surveyed the evidence for and against the view that the mother forms an attachment to her newborn infant during a relatively short sensitive post-partum period. We considered at length the numerous practical implications of the bonding view, such as birth by caesarian section, infantile autism, adoption, child abuse, and so forth. Finally, we looked at the development of maternal attachment in the light of the existing knowledge of learning processes. Throughout, we attempted to assess fairly the present state of both knowledge and ignorance with regard to maternal attachment. It is now time to see what all this adds up to.

Concern with perinatal events

We saw in Chapter 2 how infant-care practices are subject to fashions, not to say fads. It has been generally assumed that it matters a great deal how the infant is handled, and that unless it is handled correctly its future could be blighted. The plain fact is that, despite much study, there is little hard evidence concerning the relationship between specific early child rearing practices and subsequent personality development.[1] Thus, we do not really know how early breast feeding and bottle feeding compare as regards their psychological consequences, or whether, indeed, they make any difference. Likewise, we cannot be sure whether on-demand feeding is, or is not, better than feeding at fixed intervals; and we do not know whether early or late weaning make a difference to the child's personality development.

Indeed the evidence suggests that one of the crucial features of child rearing is the general social climate in the home – the attitudes, expectations and feelings of the parents which provide the backdrop to the specific methods of child care and training which they use. Mothers who do what they and the community to which they belong *believe* is right for the child are the best mothers.[2] The implication is that relaxed and confident mothers are best at mothering. However, this is difficult to achieve when 'experts' keep pointing out in great detail all the mistakes parents have made and can possibly make.[3] A burden of guilt and anxiety is thus placed on parents. We have seen the emphasis put on timing in the child-rearing literature, be it with regard to a mother making skin-to-skin contact with the child, feeding and later weaning the baby, toilet training it, and so on. Almost every member of the helping professions will recall mothers who asked whether they had done the wrong thing, made an awful mistake by doing X or neglecting to do Y or not knowing about Z, as if a single, allegedly *critical* event could leave an indelible mark on the child or the parents' relationship with the child.

The idea of critical periods implies that parents are all-powerful in their influence, all responsible, and 'must assume the role of playing preventive Fate for their children'. Yet all the available evidence gives a reassuring message to caregivers. The timing of various aspects of infant care is of very little significance.[1] And it appears that early experience, far from being *all-important*, is no more than a link in the developmental chain, shaping behaviour less and less powerfully as age increases.[4]

All this is not to say that the pattern of infant care is of no significance. The manner in which parents undertake various caregiving activities is important. As Rutter puts it:[5]

. . . feeding (whether by bottle or breast) provides a good opportunity to hold, talk to, and respond to the infant. The interaction provides experiences which influence the child's development. The art of feeding the child does more than just provide nutriment and the effect is not the same if the infant is left merely with a propped-up bottle to feed himself. *How* the baby is looked after is probably of considerable significance, but it is the social and psychosocial content of the care which matters rather than its chronology and mechanics.

Scientific knowledge can, and does, provide parents with useful guidelines for their children's development, but the eminent child psychiatrist, Hilde Bruch, is concerned that it creates an illusion of omnipotence in the area of parent education.[3] She believes that modern parent education has substituted 'scientific knowledge' for the tradition of the 'good old days'. She says 'an unrelieved picture of modern parental behaviour, a contrived image of artificial perfection and happiness is held up before parents who try valiantly to reach the ever receding ideal of "good parenthood" like dogs after a mechanical rabbit'.

Among the daunting decisions parents face is one that comes along before the baby is even born, namely the location for that particular event. Much concern has been expressed about the actual place of birth.[6] Is it to be home or hospital? The physical safety of mother and baby is a vital consideration. From that point of view the hospital provides some advantages. However, it is nowadays often said that psychologically the mother's home is the best place for confinement. Home is in very many cases a happier place than a hospital without 'rooming-in' facilities. However, in the absence of clear evidence it would be unjustified to assume that the choice of place of birth – or, indeed, the mother's position at delivery – is of crucial significance either for the psychological well-being of the mother or the development of the infant.

What emerges from cross-cultural studies of varied perinatal practices is that human beings are remarkably adaptable. It is this adaptability which has enabled the human species to survive and thrive in all sorts of situations. When it comes to making decisions about arrangements for birth and early child care, the primary consideration should be the safety and well-being of mother and baby. There is no need for mothers to feel anxious lest this or that practice will have dire psychological effects for years to come. Contrary to a variety of strongly held beliefs, there is no clear-cut evidence that events around and soon after the time of birth can readily or seriously distort either the development of the infant's personality or interfere with the growth of maternal love and attachment.

The belief in bonding

In recent years there have been many articles in magazines, Sunday papers and the like, treating rapid mother-to-infant bonding as an established fact. Such writings often derive their information from fuller, more substantial and seemingly authoritative reports. One such appeared in 1980; it is entitled *Childbirth Today*, and was published by a registered charity, called Council for Science and Society.[7] It is typical in reflecting the widespread belief in 'a sensitive period of learning for the human mother' during which she can become bonded to her newborn infant.

The report states rather boldly that 'the bonding process is largely completed within three or four days, and the contact immediately after birth is of special importance'. The significance of skin contact is mentioned. Separation at, or soon after, birth is said to be 'the commonest cause of disturbance in the bonding process'. 'The relationship of mother and infant can be seriously affected subsequently if conditions impair bonding immediately after birth.' Lack of bonding is, among other things, mentioned as a factor in child abuse.

These views are mainly based on the writings of Klaus and Kennell.[8] These writings seemed initially so convincing that many eminent developmental psychologists have accepted them without questioning. Mary Ainsworth, for instance, has recently proclaimed that 'the evidence reported so far suggests that the bonding of mother to infant may take place almost immediately after the infant's birth, provided that conditions are optimum, whereas there is every reason to believe that the attachment of infant to mother develops gradually during the infant's first six months or so of life'.[9]

Hugh Jolly, writing in the *Nursing Mirror* had advocated a close contact between mother and newborn infant in order to facilitate bonding; and, as mentioned in Chapter 5, he referred to 'disasterous consequences of separation'. However, he was clearly not accepting unquestioningly the critical-period view of bonding when he rightly stressed that 'it may take time to fall in love with your baby'.[10]

When medical and other authorities give their support to a particular theory or favour some practice, then it is well-nigh impossible for the general public to demur. After all, medical advice has often in the past been salutary. Many examples immediately spring to mind concerning such matters as hygiene, cigarette smoking and so on. But, like the rest of us, authorities and experts are not always right.

It is perhaps worth mentioning some historical cases where the prevalent medical view turned out later to be mistaken. For example, Dr William Acton, a surgeon and an authority on genito-urinary diseases in the mid-nineteenth century, described in some detail a set of symptoms which he believed to be the effects of masturbation. They were physical weakness, stunted growth, acne, and so forth. He also ascribed feeble intellect and even idiocy to masturbation (as well as to other forms of 'excessive' sexuality).[11] It has, of course, long been established that the physical and mental conditions listed by him are quite unrelated to masturbation. However, the view expressed by Dr Acton was for a long time widely believed to be valid and caused much unnecessary suffering. Some 20 years or so later, Dr J. L. H. Down described in rather precise detail a condition until recently known as mongolism, but now generally called the Down's syndrome. His descriptions of the symptoms were for the most part accurate, but some of his inter-pretations and inferences were totally wrong. One such was the view that individuals exhibiting the syndrome, whom he regarded as congenital idiots, were instances of degeneration resulting from tuberculosis in the parents.[12] Needless to say, it has been known for a long time that no such link exists. (It is now well known that the condition is due to a defective chromosome.) We should, of course, be quite unjustified in fostering general disbelief in what doctors say. On the contrary, there is good evidence that, regrettably, not enough notice is taken of doctors' instructions and advice.[13] The point of our message is simply that sometimes opinions are formed before the relevant facts are either known or thoroughly scruti-nized; and such opinions had better not become so hardened as to be impervious to contrary empirical evidence. The idea of rapid mother-to-infant bonding exemplifies well such an opinion.

The pointers of new evidence

By the late 1970s the bonding doctrine was well established and widely accepted. But the first expressions of serious doubt began to be heard at approximately the same time. In 1981 Leiderman sum-marized his own earlier investigations and stated that 'even after the initial two to three months of separation from their premature infants, mothers do establish social bonds that cannot be differen-tiated from the bonds established by the mothers of prematures and full-term mothers who initially were not separated from their in-fants'.[14] He further wrote: 'A sensitive phase, if it does exist, is at least three months in duration.' Finally he concluded that 'early contact does not necessarily facilitate social bonding; the data only suggest that this possibility exists for some individuals'.

Leiderman adopts a generally cautious view of the bonding doctrine, and suspends judgement on a number of specific issues. Yet he also writes as follows:[14]

Although the sensitive phase hypothesis does excite the imagination of ethologically oriented pediatricians, psychologists, and psychiatrists, unqualified acceptance of it can lead to the false assurance that more has actually been proven than is properly warranted. Particularly dangerous is the belief that if proper mother – infant contact is not made in the neonatal period, and if the early mother – infant bond is deficient, subsequent social bonding to other individuals is more difficult. Such a belief may encourage the premature surrender of efforts made by mothers (and fathers) to establish appropriate social bonds with their infant beyond the neonatal period. In other words, the sensitive phase hypothesis does not and should not be construed to predict later social behaviour; it can only define some of the influences upon it.

The views expressed above were strongly reinforced by a paper published in the Spring of 1982 by two eminent members of the Department of Psychiatry at the New York University Medical Center, Stella Chess and Alexander Thomas.[15] In brief, mother-to-infant bonding as currently accepted by the 'middle-class American society' – and we may add, also many professionals in Britain associated with obstetrics and paediatrics – is adjudged as 'mystique' rather than 'reality'. These authors have simply found no support for the critical-period view of bonding in the research literature. A paper published almost simultaneously by the present three authors in the *Journal of Child Psychology and Psychiatry* arrived at a similar conclusion after a searching up-to-date review of the relevant investigations.[16]

Deep scepticism about bonding conceived of as instantaneous 'glueing' is now beginning to find expression in some British professional circles. Writing in the Spring of 1982 in *Midwife, Health Visitor and Community Nurse*, Redshaw and Rosenblatt have the following to say:[17]

A contributory factor to the very real worries that parents have about the birth of their children has been the widespread emphasis, in academic and popular literature, that has been placed on the importance of 'bonding' and attachment. Many expect that this instantaneous 'glueing' will happen in the first few minutes after birth, whereas we know that it is usually a more gradual process occurring over the course of several days or weeks in the post-natal period, or even longer. The evidence for an extremely short 'critical' period in human parents is inconclusive to say the least, and the guilt and anxiety which may result from such high expectations being un-fulfilled are an unnecessary burden. Parents and infants are considerably more resilient and flexible than they are often given credit for, as is evi-denced in their ability to cope with very different experiences of birth. For instance, after a caesarean section or pre-term delivery there is usually little chance for the highly recommended immediate post-partum contact and the separation which follows birth is a physical one and not just psychological. Though there may be problems for such families this does not inevitably mean a damaged relationship and emotional scarring of parents and infant for life. Of course, this is not to suggest that the possibilities for early contact between parents and their babies should not be increased or encouraged. Nor does it mean that the effects of new and established procedures and modes of delivery on the mother and infant should remain uninvestigated.

A few practical suggestions

Throughout the world human beings are born and flourish in a great variety of situations. In view of this adaptability the reader may come to feel that it does not much matter whether the mother and her newborn infant have, or have not, skin contact, whether they are, or are not, temporarily separated, and so forth. Perhaps altogether too much fuss is made in criticizing the bonding doc-trine; perhaps the doctrine, even if unsound, is harmless enough. The evidence indicates that the actual perinatal arrangements are not crucial, as such. Nevertheless what the mother believes with regard to such matters as contact and separation, the sensitive period, and bonding in general, is important.

Her beliefs are important because they may make her fearful and influence her behaviour, perhaps for years to come, towards her offspring. This, in turn, may influence the personality development of her child or children. The risk is that the influence could be an adverse one, though the degree of risk cannot be readily evaluated and should not be over-emphasized. In any case, any unnecessary anxiety engendered in the mother is clearly undesirable. Thus, it is of considerable importance that no misconceptions be entertained by doctors, nurses and, above all, parents about maternal bonding.

It is vitally important to remember that the factors that influence a child's behaviour and development over time are many-sided and very complex. It is generally a good idea to treat apparently simple explanations of complicated behaviour patterns with a degree of scepticism or, at least, caution. This caveat applies particularly to the attempt to reduce complex problems to *single* causes, a feature, of course, of the bonding hypothesis.

Hinde illustrates well the significant features of family life which have to be assessed when considering causal outcomes.[18] The child has a relationship with each and every member of the family so that father – child and sibling – sibling interactions and relationships must be considered in addition to those of the mother and child. Then again, relationships always involve mutual influences; children influence their parents and are not simply the ones being influenced. Relationships affect each other; thus the mother – child relationship is affected by the relationship between the parents. How one parent conducts himself or herself with the children is influenced by the presence or absence of the spouse.

The family is not static; it changes over the years; and, of course, family life is not impervious to outside social conditions and influences. Hinde also makes the important point that to a considerable extent relationships and structures are self-regulatory. As a result, an influence that appears to be significant in the short-term may be unimportant in the longer run.

The birth of a baby is a great event in the mother's life – in some ways, a crisis. It is then that she needs a support network – the father of her child, her family and friends, a sympathetic midwife, and understanding doctor perhaps, and so on. In the best of circumstances she will be a little anxious lest something goes wrong. What she does not need is extra worry.

In view of what is now known, no mother should worry if she initially feels no love for her baby, even after repeated skin-to-skin contact has occurred. Mothers' feelings do not follow a stereotype. Warm feelings of attachment to the baby are sometimes quick to come and sometimes very slow. Being able to respond to the baby's basic needs is a sign that the attachment process is under way, even though the mother may feel uncertain about it.

In those unfortunate cases where safety considerations require that the child be removed from the mother at birth or shortly thereafter, social workers and those concerned with legal proceedings need not worry about maternal bonding when a statutory removal of a newborn infant from its natural mother is carried out.

Adherents of the bonding doctrine believe that, once the infant is taken away at birth, it is inadvisable ever to return it to the mother, even when circumstances allow it, because the mother has not been bonded to her baby and so can never be a really good mother.[19] When these problems arise, any consideration of bonding is irrelevant, and can make the decision more difficult to reach. Equally, if the baby is taken away from its natural mother not shortly after birth but weeks or months later, the question of bonding should not be a worry to the social worker. Whether the child settles well or badly in its new environment will depend on a host of factors, but again, maternal bonding is not a relevant consideration.

To bond or not to bond – that is the question that often exercises nurses in maternity hospitals. Some nurses are said to encourage 'bonding' in mothers who will shortly have their babies taken away for ever,[20] and they are criticized for it. One could equally criticize nurses who attempt to 'bond' mothers to their to-be-kept newborn infants by enforcing skin-to-skin and other forms of contact irrespective of the circumstances and the mothers' inclinations. There is no need for nurses or mothers to attach any special importance to skin contact. Nurses may do what seems sensible in the given circumstances. The aim is, of course, to be kind to the mother; but being kind will mean much contact in some cases and little contact in others. Everything should depend on what suits best all concerned; the mother, the infant, the father, the nurse, and so on.

Our message to the mother who harbours secret fears, lest she has not been properly bonded to her infant is 'Stop worrying, your anxiety is the result of your acceptance of the bonding doctrine. It was perfectly sensible of you to believe it when no-one knew better; but we now know that research findings reveal no critical period for maternal bonding, and these findings strongly indicate that maternal attachment – like child-to-adult attachment – develops in most cases slowly but surely.'

References

1   Caldwell, B.M. (1964) 'The effects of infant care'. In Hoffman, M.L. and Hoffman, L.W. (eds) *Review of Child Development Research,* Vol. 1 (New York: Russell Sage Foundation).
    Lee, S.G.M. and Herbert, M. (eds) (1970) *Freud and Psychology* (London: Penguin Books).

2 Behrens, M.L. (1954) 'Child rearing and the character structure of the mother', *Child Development*, **25**, 225 – 38.

3 Bruch, H. (1954) 'Parent education or the illusion of omnipotence', *American Journal of Orthopsychiatry*, **24**, 273 – 4.

4 Clarke, A.M. and Clarke, A.D.B. (1976) *Early Experience: Myth and Evidence* (London: Open Books).

5 Rutter, M. (1977) 'Other family influences'. In Rutter, M. and Hersov, L. (eds) *Child Psychiatry: Modern Approaches* (Oxford: Blackwell Scientific Publications).

6 Kitzinger, S. and Davis, J.A. (eds) (1978) *The Place of Birth* (Oxford: Oxford University Press).

7 *Childbirth Today* 1980 (London: Council for Science and Society).

8 Klaus, M.H. and Kennell, J.H. (1976) *Maternal – infant Bonding* (St Louis: Mosby).

9 Ainsworth, M.D.S. (1982) 'Attachment: retrospect and prospect'. In Parkes, C.M. and Stevenson-Hinde, J. (eds), *The Place of Attachment in Human Behavior* (London: Tavistock).

10 Jolly, H. (1978) 'The importance of "bonding" for newborn baby, mother . . . and father', *Nursing Mirror*, 31 August, 19 – 21.

11 Marcus, S. (1966) *The Other Victorians: A Study of Sexuality and Pornography in Mid-Nineteenth Century England* (London: Weidenfeld & Nicolson).

12 Pappworth, M. (1982) 'Was Down a racist?', *World Medicine*. **17**, No. 12, 59.

13 Peck, D. (1978) 'Communications and compliance', *Bulletin of the British Psychological Society*, **31**, 348 – 52.

14 Leiderman, P. (1981) 'Human mother – infant social bonding: is there a sensitive phase?' In Immelmann, K., Barlow, G.W., Petrinovich, L. and Main, M. (eds) *Behavioral Development* (Cambridge: Cambridge University Press).

15 Chess, S. and Thomas, A. (1982) 'Infant bonding: mystique and reality', *American Journal of Orthopsychiatry*, **52**, 213 – 22.

16 Herbert, M., Sluckin, W. and Sluckin, A. (1982) 'Mother-to-infant "bonding"', *Journal of Child Psychology and Psychiatry*, **23**, 205 – 21.

17 Redshaw, M. and Rosenblatt, D.B. (1982) 'The influence of analgesia in labour on the baby', *Midwife, Health Visitor and Community Nurse*, **18**, 126 – 32.

18 Hinde, R.A. (1979) 'Family influences'. In Rutter, M. (ed.) *Scientific Foundations of Developmental Psychiatry* (London: Heinemann).

19 Tredinnick, A.W. and Fairburn, A.C. (1980) 'The baby removed from its parents at birth – prophylaxis with justice?', *New Law Journal*, **130**, 498 – 500.

20 Fairburn, A.C. and Tredinnick, A.W. (1980) 'Babies removed from their parents at birth. 160 statutory care actions', *British Medical Journal*, **280**, 987 – 91.

Index